startup

Start Your Own

BUSINESS SUPPORT SERVICE

Your Step-by-Step Guide to Success

Jacquelyn Lynn

EP
Entrepreneur.
Press

Editorial Director: Jere L. Calmes
Managing Editor: Marla Markman
Cover Design: Beth Hansen-Winter
Production: Eliot House Productions
Composition: Patricia Miller

This publication is designed to provide accurate and authoritative information in regard to
the subject matter covered. It is sold with the understanding that the publisher is not
engaged in rendering legal, accounting, or other professional services. If legal advice or
other expert assistance is required, the services of a competent professional person should be
sought.

Library of Congress Cataloging-in-Publication Data
Lynn, Jacquelyn.
    Start your own business support service/by Jacquelyn Lynn.
      p.   cm.   —(Entrepreneur magazine's start up) (Entrepreneur magazine's
business start-up series; #1136)
    Includes index.
    ISBN 1-891984-84-5
    1. Business consultants. 2. New business enterprises—Management. I. Title:
Business support service. II. Entrepreneur (Santa Monica, Calif.) III. Title. IV. Series.
V. Entrepreneur business start-up guide; no. 1136.

HD69.C6 L957 2003
001'.068'1—dc21   2002192766

Printed in Canada

09 08 07 06 05 04 03   10 9 8 7 6 5 4 3 2 1

Contents

▲

Preface

Business is becoming more complex every day, and the tools we use to run our companies are becoming increasingly sophisticated. This is creating tremendous opportunities for the business support services industry.

Other factors contributing to the growth of business support services include the increasing number of small businesses and homebased businesses, and the trend of outsourcing noncore business tasks. It just doesn't make sense for small companies to hire someone with every skill they need, especially when those skills are readily available from other small companies that specialize in various support-type services.

Consider a business that wants to send out a quarterly newsletter. It can purchase desktop-publishing software and a high-end laser printer and hire a staff writer and graphic designer (paying salary, benefits, etc.) to do what amounts to a few hours of work four times a year. Or they can contract with a business support services company to do a comparable job and pay only for the services they use. Which makes more sense?

Maybe a business needs tapes transcribed. Should it hire a typist and buy transcription equipment, or send the tapes out to a service that can do it for them? Or what about when a business has a short-term special project that needs to be done but doesn't have the staff available to do it? Should it hire for the short term or outsource to a business support service? And then there's the homebased business owner who needs secretarial work done but doesn't have the physical space to hire someone to come in and work, even on a part-time basis—a business support service company may be the answer.

Small businesses are not the only customers of business support services. Large corporations also regularly use them to outsource routine tasks and special projects. Individuals are also a substantial customer group: students who need term papers typed; job seekers who need professional-looking resumes; writers who need help with typing, editing, and manuscript preparation; and more. Given this variety of potential clients, a business support service firm can successfully operate in just about any part of the country and in communities of all sizes.

Another lure of the business support service industry is the diversity it offers operators. You can do it part time or full time. You can specialize in one or two particular services or offer a wide range of services from basic word processing to database management to desktop publishing. You can earn a comfortable income working from home as a solo operator, or you can set up in a commercial location with employees. You can work successfully with a basic computer and printer, or you can invest in an array of high-tech equipment.

Regardless of the particular type of business you want to start, this book will tell you how to do it. We'll start with an overview of the industry, look at the services you'll want to consider offering, and then go through the step-by-step process of setting up and running your new venture.

So limber up your fingers, because when you've finished this book, you'll be ready to make your computer sing an exciting and profitable song of new business.

1

More Than
Typing

The secretary of yesteryear needed to know how to take shorthand, type, and answer the phone. Today's secretary deals with dictation using a tape recorder and transcription equipment; instead of simply typing, she inputs data into a small but powerful computer; and the office telephone she uses is actually a complex communications center.

▲

What we now call the business support services industry has experienced a similar and perhaps even more remarkable evolution. It began as secretarial services or typing services, and typing was pretty much all they did. But those operations have gone the way of the horse and buggy, replaced by modern, techno-savvy entrepreneurs who want to take advantage of a virtually limitless market.

Though the term "secretarial service" has a strong degree of consumer recognition, it's no longer an appropriate description of the industry. While typing and transcription (historically typical secretarial services) are still a mainstay, consumers often don't think of a secretarial service as providing desktop publishing, spreadsheet design, Internet-related services, and other sophisticated product and service packages. The phrase "business support services" does a much better job of conveying what the industry is all about today and still leaves flexibility for the changes that are likely to occur in the future. You'll also hear terms such as "administrative support services" and "office support services" applied to this industry.

In 1998, the National Association of Secretarial Services changed its name to the Association of Business Support Services International Inc. (ABSSI). Executive Director Lynette M. Smith says, "We felt that 'business support services' did a better job than 'secretarial services' of covering the scope of our members' services and bringing more respectability to the profession."

Of course, the size of the market for business support services is difficult to estimate for a number of reasons—primarily because the U.S. Bureau of the Census mixes other types of businesses with business support services. Also, the providers, services, and customers are constantly evolving with technological advances. The secretarial service of the 1960s and 1970s, when a good electric typewriter was pretty much all you needed, wouldn't get off the ground today. And who knows what technology will be able to do 20 or 30 years from now?

Another issue to keep in mind is that the business support service industry is typically not subject to seasonal fluctuations. Operators report a slight slowdown in the summer and again during the Christmas holiday season—but that gives them a break so they can take their own vacations and enjoy the holidays without having to inconvenience their clients.

As a business support service owner, be prepared for the reality that the company you start today will likely bear little resemblance to the one you'll be running in five or ten years. But as long as you pay attention to what's going on in the market and stay flexible, your chances of having a strong, profitable operation are excellent.

Who Are the Players?

Who is likely to start a business support service company? Today's owners were employees doing similar tasks for other companies and saw the opportunity to be in business for themselves. Some wanted full-time businesses; others were looking for a solid part-time income source.

Charlene D. is a classic example: She had been a full-time legal assistant when she started her part-time homebased business in Winter Park, Florida. Her goal was to have more time and flexibility to be at home with her newly, adopted son, but to not completely give up her career and income. In fact, one of her key challenges is keeping her business part-time and small. "I could easily turn it into a big business because I've gotten a lot of referrals and I turn down a lot of work," she says. "Fortunately, I don't [need] the income, and I prefer to keep my hours light. I choose when and when not to work, and I keep my client list very short and manageable."

Stat Fact
According to the U.S. Department of Labor, as an industry, computer and data processing services is expected to grow nearly 108 percent between 1996 and 2006, making it the fastest-growing industry in America.

Like Charlene, Rachelle Y., of Perrysburg, Ohio, wanted to be able to work from home, spend time with her children, and still make a decent income. She considered buying the secretarial service where she had worked but, after doing some research, she decided to start her own homebased business instead. "I'm not in it to make a huge amount of money," she says. She enjoys working on the computer, staying current with new technology, and earning enough money to supplement her husband's income.

As a secretary for the Oklahoma Small Business Development Center (SBDC), Janet S. had spent years watching others start and build businesses. In addition to her

Sit this One Out

If you have small children and you're starting a homebased business support service, don't try to do it without a sitter. You won't be able to concentrate on your work if you're also listening for the kids. To be fair to yourself, your company, your clients, and your children, arrange for someone to watch the youngsters while you're working and meeting with clients.

"You can always run errands with the children in tow—it may take longer, but it's not a real hardship," says Charlene D., the Winter Park, Florida, homebased entrepreneur. "But when you're actually working on projects, you need time to do it uninterrupted, when you can really focus on the job itself."

Keep in mind that if you're going to be at home working within earshot of the kids, you can hire a younger, less experienced, less expensive sitter than you might hire if you were going to be out.

▲

day job, she had also been typing papers for college students from her home in Edmond, which meant the transition to business support service owner would be a natural one. She had been thinking about starting her own business when the office she worked in was damaged in the 1995 bombing of the Federal Building in Oklahoma City. The SBDC moved to a temporary location, and Janet stayed in her position and was eventually promoted, but recovering from the trauma of the bombing was difficult. "The longer I waited for things to return to 'normal,' the further and further I sunk into depression," she recalls. "The harder I tried to bring myself out of the depression, the deeper I went. I finally decided the only choice I had was to quit." The change kicked her out of her depression and into a successful business.

In contrast to these homebased operators, Cindy P.'s business support service in Irvine, California, targets the legal field, and her commercial office is bursting at the seams with herself and three employees (in addition, she has one employee who works from home). She had been working in a law office but was bored because there wasn't enough work to keep her busy. She was looking for another job when she learned of a secretarial service that was for sale. She bought the business, and now she's evaluating various expansion options.

Joann V. began doing transcribing for court reporters at night to supplement her income from her full-time office manager's job. "I became overwhelmed with how much outside work I was getting, so I quit my job and started doing this full time," she says. That was in 1984; today, her Chicago company specializes in audiotape and videotape transcription, and does work for clients across the country.

Bill P.'s path to owning a business support service was less traditional. His wife actually started the business he now runs in Iowa City, Iowa. She was successfully working from home, and after their second child was born, Bill began helping her while he attended graduate school. When their third child came along, she opened a homebased day-care center, and Bill took over the business support service and moved it into a commercial office.

Though their businesses vary by location and services provided, the common thread among these operators is that they all did the type of work involved before they actually began running their own company. This explains one of the biggest challenges of starting and running a business support service: the need to go beyond pure technical skills and understand how to manage and grow a business. That's what this book is all about.

The Sky's the Limit

Is there a lot of opportunity in the business support service industry? "There's so much—there's an incredible amount of business out there," says Cindy P.

To understand the future potential, take a look at how the industry has evolved. Over the span of the 20th century, the administrative demands of doing business have

Profit Prophet

A business support service is not a get-rich-quick operation. Like most legitimate businesses, it takes dedication, hard work, and a lot of time to build a profitable company. But with a well-thought-out, enthusiastic marketing plan, you'll probably see your income exceed your cumulative expenses three to 12 months after opening your doors. How much you'll ultimately make depends on how hard you're willing to work, how many hours you put in, and the type of business (small, one-person shop, or larger operation with employees) you start.

If you work alone, keep in mind that you'll only be able to bill about 75 percent of your available business hours—the rest of your time will be spent marketing, doing your own administrative work, and on other nonbillable tasks. And even though you can get "out of the red" fairly quickly in this business, it could take a year or more before you are actually working full time on clients' projects.

grown tremendously, creating a need for secretarial and clerical support. With the advent of desktop computers and increasingly sophisticated office equipment, the skill and knowledge requirements of secretaries have also increased.

At the same time, the general business landscape has changed dramatically. Big businesses are looking for ways to streamline their operations, and one popular option is outsourcing, where they retain another company to provide a service that may have traditionally been done by employees. Small companies want to stay lean and profitable, so they, too, are turning to outsourcing, rather than fattening up their payroll. (See Chapter 4 for more about who uses business support services and why.)

Combine the obvious need with the new way of operating in the business world, and you have a dynamic young industry wide-open with opportunity: business support services. In fact, there is so much opportunity that if you don't have a clear plan, specific services, and a target market, your chances of success are slim. But with a lot of thought and preparation, and a minimal amount of cash, you can quickly be on the road to profitability.

After you decide to get into the business, one of the next choices you're going to have to make is whether to start your own company or buy an existing concern.

Making the Choice

Owning a business support service doesn't necessarily require building the company from scratch. You might want to consider buying an existing business, especially if the appeal of being in business for yourself is in *running* the company rather than *starting* it.

This alternative route to business ownership has some advantages worth considering. It allows you to bypass all the steps involved in creating a business infrastructure because the original owner has already done that. You can take over an operation that is already generating cash flow—and perhaps even profits. You'll have a history on which to build your forecasts and a future that includes an established customer base. And there's generally less risk involved in buying an existing concern than there is in creating a whole new company.

Beware!

Don't be a victim of a scam. You'll see plenty of ads out there that promise you can make lots of money working from home on your computer. Sadly, many of these offers are scams that ask you to send money you'll never recoup. Be a smart consumer: If something sounds too good to be true, it probably is.

Of course, there are drawbacks to buying a business. Though the actual dollar amounts depend on the size and type of business, it often takes more cash to buy an existing business than to start one yourself. When you buy a company's assets, you'll usually get stuck with at least some of the liabilities. And it's highly unlikely that you'll find an existing business that is precisely the company you would have built on your own. Even so, you just might find that the business you want is currently owned by someone else.

Why do people sell businesses—especially profitable ones? For a variety of reasons. Many entrepreneurs are happiest during the start-up and early growth stages of a company; once the business is running smoothly, they get bored and begin looking for something new. Other business owners may grow tired of the responsibility, or be facing health or other personal issues that motivate them to sell their companies. In fact, some of the most successful entrepreneurs go into business with a solid plan for how they're going to get out of the business when the time comes.

If you decide to shop around for an existing business support service, look at *every* service provider in the area that meets your requirements; just because it isn't on the market doesn't mean it isn't for sale. Use your networking skills to find potential companies; let friends and colleagues know what you're looking for. You might even consider placing a "wanted to buy" classified ad.

Evaluating a Company

One of the most challenging financial calculations is figuring out what a business is worth. You may want to take the time to research the selling price and terms of recently sold companies in the industry, and use them as a guide. Or you may value the company based on its after-tax cash flow, or on the value of the company's assets, if they were liquidated, minus the debts and liabilities. You should call on your financial advisors to assist you with working through these calculations.

The figures are only part of the equation. Elements that are not as easy to assign a value to include the company's reputation and the strength of the relationship the current owner has with customers, suppliers, and employees.

Thorough due diligence is an essential part of the acquisition process. This includes reviewing, auditing, and verifying all the relevant information regarding the business—and doing it means you'll know exactly what you are buying and from whom. Have your accountant assist you in evaluating the financial statements, your banker help with financing issues, and your attorney guide you in researching the legal aspects. And remember that you can walk away from the deal at any point in the negotiation process before a contract is signed.

Rachelle Y. was working for a secretarial service when she found out the owner was interested in selling the company. At first, she thought it was a tremendous opportunity. "I essentially ran the company, except for the financial end," she recalls. "I knew the customers, and I did all the work. I thought that, with the established clients and the equipment package, it would be a sure thing." Then she found out that the owner was asking more for the equipment than she had paid for it. "Equipment depreciates, and she wanted me to pay more than it had cost her. That made me leery of the whole situation." She backed out of the deal, found another job, and eventually started her own company.

Cindy P. has another example of why thorough due diligence is so critical. The business she bought "was portrayed to me as a very large business that made an incredible amount of money," she recalls. "We looked at the books, and everything seemed fine—however, things were not as they claimed." The business was not generating the revenue indicated in the records Cindy examined, and she ended up having to virtually restart the business from scratch. She considered suing the seller for fraud and misrepresentation but decided instead to focus her energy and resources on building her new business.

The process was a tremendous learning experience, though. If she were to do it again,

▲

she would use a business broker to assist with the research and negotiations, and verify the accuracy of the records by checking outside sources.

Going It on Your Own

Though buying an existing business may be a good way to enter the industry, most business support service owners start their own companies. This way, you can choose the exact services you want to offer, define the market you want to serve, and do things your way from the start.

Let's begin by taking a look at the tremendous range of services you can offer.

2

Services and
Policies

The mainstay of the business support service
industry is word processing, and there was a time when many
businesses could survive offering that alone. But as computer
prices drop, software becomes easier to use, and more people
learn to type, people who were prospective clients of secretarial
services a decade ago are now doing much of their own

correspondence, reports, and presentations. Even though there will likely always be plenty of word-processing work out there and you can make this the foundation of your business, you need to diversify into other specialty areas.

"While word processing is a good core service, it's vital for the new business owner to diversify into at least two other higher-end specialties, such as desktop publishing, Web site design, Internet research, event planning, and so on," says Lynette M. Smith, executive director of the Association of Business Support Services International Inc. (ABSSI). "I am firmly convinced that the new business owner can't make a go of it with word processing alone."

Iowa City, Iowa, entrepreneur Bill P. agrees. He believes there will always be a market for word processing, but as more people become computer-literate and as technologies such as speech recognition make computer use even easier, that market will likely shrink; you need to have a plan for other options. "There will always be something that's a little more complicated to do," he says. "You have to find new markets."

So what services should you offer? That's a decision you'll make based on your own individual skills, your personal preferences, and your goals for your company. If you're planning to stay small and do most of the work yourself, you'll want to specialize in services you enjoy and do well. If you plan to assemble a team of workers with a variety of skills, you can offer a much broader scope of services. Here's what the business owners we talked with offer:

- Charlene D. in Winter Park, Florida, primarily does word processing and desktop publishing. She produces an association newsletter and manages that client's membership database, and also does tape transcription and other administrative support work for her clients.

- Perrysburg, Ohio's Rachelle Y. does what she calls "secretarial work." She explains, "I subcontract for any company that is looking for a secretary but does not want to hire someone on a full-time basis."

- Bill P. says the majority of his business is resumes, but he also does a substantial amount of transcription, along with word processing dissertations for graduate students and some work for small businesses and independent sales representatives who work out of their homes.

- Janet S. in Edmond, Oklahoma, does word processing, database and mailing list management, bulk mailing preparation, presentations, correspondence, and machine transcription for small-business owners, attorneys, professional organizations, churches, and college students.

- Joann V. in Chicago targets two primary markets: insurance and television production. For the insurance market, she transcribes recorded statements by people who have been involved in car accidents. Her other main market is television production companies that need audiotape and videotape transcription.

Business Support Services

You can offer a wide range of services. The following list encompasses what we found on the market, but it is by no means exhaustive. Some of these services could be businesses in and of themselves; others are ancillary to a primary service. Listen to your clients; they'll let you know what they need, and then you can decide if you can provide it.

- *Word processing.* This is a service in itself, as well as a component of other services you may provide. Essentially, it's the task of creating documents in an electronic format, manipulating them according to your clients' needs, and then outputting them to paper or another electronic format. Word processing is the one service that all business support services have in common.

- *Tape transcription.* Businesses and individuals frequently need a hard-copy transcript of material on audiotape or videotape. It could be a speech, lecture, interview, or radio or television show. You may also have clients who provide you with taped dictation, and you transcribe the material and follow the instructions they give you. Legal and medical transcription are two specialty areas that require familiarity with the professions, terminology, and formatting requirements. For more on transcription services, see Entrepreneur's business start-up guide No. 1392, *Medical Transcription Service.*

- *Phone-in dictation.* If you're going to offer transcription, you may want to set up a system where clients can dictate over the phone into a special system that stores their words either on tape or electronically. You then transcribe their dictation as you would if it had been supplied to you on tape.

- *Desktop publishing.* This is another phrase that is becoming almost as broad as "word processing" in its scope. It can include anything from simple page design to complicated graphics work. Most word-processing software packages have the capability of basic desktop publishing, although if you're going to do multicolor brochures or large projects, you'll probably want to invest in either QuarkXPress or PageMaker, the two most popular desktop-publishing programs on the market. For more on the subject, check out Entrepreneur's business start-up guide No. 1288, *Desktop Publishing Business.*

- *Spreadsheet design.* Spreadsheets are the electronic version of the old bookkeeping ledger pages, and technology

> **Tip...**
>
> **Smart Tip**
>
> If you realize you've underestimated your workload and you're likely going to miss a deadline, call the client as soon as possible, apologize, and give them a realistic estimate of when the work is going to be done. Don't let them show up at your office to pick up a job that isn't finished.

has made them an extremely useful business tool. You may have clients who need information arranged in a spreadsheet, but do not have the equipment, skills, or time to design the document or input the data.

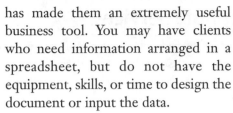

Smart Tip

Limit the number of no-charge revisions you'll do on a desktop-publishing project. Certainly you won't charge for correcting any mistakes you may have made that the client catches, but if the client keeps making design changes after approving the initial plan, you should be compensated for your time.

- *College paper/report preparation.* Students at both the undergraduate and graduate levels often turn to professionals to type and format their theses, dissertations, and other important projects. Universities can be extremely particular in how these documents are formatted, and many students don't have the time or inclination to figure out how to do it right, so they're willing to pay someone to do it for them. The schools publish instructions and often even sell a software template with the correct formatting; contact the university for details on how to get this information. Some students may ask you to edit their papers; Bill P. says he does this only when the student has the professor's permission.

- *Telephone answering.* Even though voice mail is a popular and accepted communication tool, many businesses still prefer their phone to be answered by a live person, but they don't need a full-time receptionist. You can answer their phone, take messages, and/or route calls into a voice-mail system. Consult with your telephone company for information on the necessary equipment and setup costs.

- *Mail receiving and forwarding.* Clients without a commercial office and clients who are on the road frequently need a service that will accept their mail and packages, and either hold it for them or forward it to wherever they happen to be. You can set up a simple system for sorting and storing your clients' mail, or you can put up mailboxes like those used by the United States Postal Service (USPS).

- *Packing and shipping.* You may handle packing items and shipping parcels through a variety of ground and over-night carriers, such as UPS, Airborne, Federal Express, the USPS, and others. You'll charge your client a small handling fee. Also, you may receive a discount from the carriers that you can absorb as your profit or pass along to your clients.

- *Database/mailing list management.* Small businesses or independent sales reps often need to maintain computer databases of customers and prospects, and often need to outsource this task. There are a number of user-friendly contact-management software packages on the market that will work for this function.

- *Bookkeeping, check preparation, and billing.* Most small businesses don't need a full-time bookkeeper, but they do need someone to maintain their financial records, generate invoices, and prepare checks. You can do this for your clients using an off-the-shelf business accounting software package.

- *Resume preparation.* Your service in this area can range from simply typing and formatting the information provided by the client to working closely with the client to develop the content of the resume. Some people believe the latter falls more in the area of career counseling, which you may also want to do.

- *Proofreading.* This can involve comparing a new document against an original to be sure they are the same or reading a document and checking for spelling, grammar, and punctuation mistakes.

- *Print brokering.* Some of the work you'll do for clients will be sent to a printer for volume reproduction. You can help out your clients and add to your own revenue by functioning as a broker on the printing; you do the shopping and get the best price, quality, and service package, and then supervise the project for your client. You'll earn a commission from the printer for your efforts.

- *Fax sending and receiving.* Though most businesses have fax machines, you may have clients who are either new, very small, or individuals who need to send and receive faxes. You may also want to provide broadcast fax services for clients.

- *Photocopying.* Even though your clients may own their own photocopying machines, they may still need you to make copies for them. Also, if you're in a commercial location, you may get some walk-in traffic for copy services.

- *Notarizing.* You can notarize signatures for your clients and provide other notary services as your state's laws permit; this is especially helpful for commercial-based operations that might also get some walk-in clients.

- *Internet research.* You may have clients who need data but don't have time to find it. With the vast amount of information available on the Internet, you can do the research for them.

- *Web page design and maintenance.* You could design Web pages and handle updates and changes for your clients. For more on this topic, see Entrepreneur's business start-up guide No. 1237, *Information Broker.*

- *Event planning.* Meeting and party planning is a business field of its own, but you may be able to help your

Bright Idea

Set your rush rate at a percentage above your regular fee. For example, Joann V. in Chicago charges 30 percent above her regular rate for rush jobs; Cindy P. in Irvine, California, charges 50 percent more for work clients want back in less than 24 hours.

▲

"I Do" or "I Don't"?

You don't have to accept every project a client brings you. Here are some questions to ask to help you decide when to say yes—and when to say no.

○ *Will you enjoy the work?* If you're a solo operator and will be doing the work yourself, is it something you'll enjoy, or will you be miserable?

○ *Do you have time to do the job right?* Consider this from two angles: Do you want to spend the time, and can you meet the deadline?

○ *Will accepting this particular job (or taking on this client) affect your relationship with existing clients?*

○ *Is there anything questionable about the work in terms of honesty, integrity, or legality?*

clients with small events and meetings, particularly if your office has conference space available. For more information, check out Entrepreneur's business start-up guide No. 1313, *Event Planning Service.*

- *Consulting.* This covers a wide range of issues and will depend on your particular areas of expertise. For example, you may be able to work with a client in getting his or her own office set up, equipped, and properly staffed. When you work with a client in a problem-solving or advisory capacity, you should be paid for your time as a consultant. For more on this topic, see Entrepreneur's *Start Your Own Consulting Service.*

- *Training.* In the process of providing your services, you have probably gained a significant amount of expertise in the hardware and software you use, and there's no reason you shouldn't train others to use the same equipment and be paid for that service.

Most business support services offer pickup and delivery. If you're a solo operator, you'll probably just use your personal car to handle this chore. Or you may use a courier service.

Should you charge for pickup and delivery? That's a judgment call you'll have to make; some operators do, and some don't. Charlene D., for example, doesn't charge for pickup and delivery because her clients are within a few miles' radius of her house, and she combines this task with other errands, so she doesn't feel that it's taking a significant amount of time.

Rachelle Y. makes the decision on a per-client basis. But if you're going to charge, she cautions, be sure you charge enough. She had one client who agreed to pay her travel time, but she underestimated how long it actually took to make the drive, and that mistake reduced her profitability.

Also, as part of your overall service package, you may want to maintain an inventory of basic office supplies and perhaps even specialty papers that you can either use in the process of doing your clients' work or that you may actually sell outright to them. You can purchase these products in bulk from wholesalers to allow room for a reasonable markup when you sell individual items.

Certainly you won't have the volume to compete with your local office supply house, but you may still want to sell products such as pens, markers, labels, computer disks, paper, and envelopes. You may also want to keep a stock or a catalog of specialty papers for small runs of brochures or special mailings as a cost-effective alternative to four-color, large-quantity printing. Your clients may also appreciate being able to purchase postage stamps from you, rather than having to make a trip to the post office.

Making the Rules

In any relationship, it's a good idea to set boundaries so everyone knows what to expect before any problems develop. In business, those boundaries are usually couched in the form of policies. How formal you want to be will depend on your own personal preferences, the size of your business, and your clientele. Charlene D. takes a casual approach to polices, simply giving new clients a verbal explanation of how she operates. Her relationship with her clients is very personal, and while she always does her best to meet their needs, it isn't always possible. "I'm a one-person company, and I don't pretend to be anything else," she says. "When I get a project, I find out when the deadline is, and if I can't meet it, I say so. It may be because I've got other work to do, or I may have personal obligations—whatever. I just say, 'I'm sorry, but I'm not going to be able to turn that around for you in that time frame.' Then we decide if they can live with what I can do, or if they need to take the job somewhere else."

Cindy P. in Irvine, California, takes a more structured approach, providing each new client with a written policy statement that clearly outlines what she will and won't do. (For an example, turn to page 17.) She developed the policy statement after an unfortunate experience with a client who wanted her to retrieve a significant number of files but did not want to pay for the time it would take or the disks Cindy would have to provide. The client eventually sued, and

> **Tip...**
>
> **Smart Tip**
> Whatever services you offer, be sure you do top-quality work. Pay attention to details, meet your deadlines, and be sure the final product is error-free.

▲

although Cindy won, she realized the entire situation could have been prevented with a policy statement.

Policies also give your clients some guidelines so that they can make reasonable requests. Many clients seem excessively demanding because they just don't think about what's involved in getting the work done; setting policies that give them choices in pricing and service levels will make your relationship smoother and stronger.

"Implementing time frame policies and rush policies has helped so much," says Cindy. "People don't think. They drop something off in the afternoon and expect it back first thing in the morning. We'll do that, but they have to pay time and a half for it. When they find out that if they want something in less than 24 hours they have to pay more for it, all of a sudden they don't need it so fast."

Though consistency in applying policies is important, so is using good judgment. "Obviously, if it's my biggest client and they want a label typed in a hurry, they'll get it," Cindy says. "But I'll be the one to make that decision."

Policy Statement

ABC Secretarial Service

1. Standard turnaround time is 24 to 48 hours. (Some projects may require additional time, which will be decided and agreed upon at the time of project drop-off.)

2. Rush rates are available. Any project required in less than 24 hours will be billed at a 50 percent increase.

3. A minimum charge of .5 hours (1/2 hour) will always apply.

4. Time spent with client discussing or reviewing the project will be applicable to ABC Secretarial Service's hourly rate.

5. Payment for all projects is required at time of pickup. If monthly billing is requested, a credit form is available. Monthly billing will not be available until credit references are verified and credit is approved.

6. We will make every effort to locate and correct all errors prior to your review; however, **CLIENT** is responsible for final proof. Our responsibility is limited to providing you with original page(s) only and does not extend to duplicating charges. Therefore, proofread your project carefully **PRIOR** to duplication. Errors or omissions found thereafter are **CLIENT'S** responsibility.

7. Should an electronic copy of your project be required, a five-dollar ($5) fee per document, plus a "disk" charge, will be applied. (Disk charges vary depending on the type of disk required.)

8. ABC's files will be purged one year after completion of project. Should you require longer storage, arrangements must be made in advance and a storage fee will be applied. Should a client return after a project has been purged and storage arrangements have not been made, client shall then be responsible for charges incurred to rekey the entire document.

9. Prices are subject to change without prior notice.

10. All typeset and print work must be signed off by client. Should an error in typesetting be found after print is run, **CLIENT** will be responsible for reprint charges.

If you have any questions regarding the above policies,
please do not hesitate to contact us.
Thank you for choosing ABC Secretarial Service.

Day-to-Day
Operations

Most people start a particular type of business because they enjoy doing that kind of work, and the typical business support service owner is no different. So you may find it frustrating that a major portion of your time will be spent on tasks other than doing projects for your clients.

Photo© PhotoDisc Inc.

In fact, it will be common for you to have days that are extremely busy and you work very hard, but you don't do anything that can be billed to a client.

As a solo operator, expect to spend at least one-fourth of your time on general business management and administration, marketing, purchasing, and billing. The bigger your business, and the more workers you have, the more time you'll spend managing them rather than actually doing the work yourself. With four employees, Irvine, California's Cindy P. spends very little of her time working on projects for clients. And Chicago entrepreneur Joann V. hasn't actually transcribed anything herself in years—she has a team of five full-time employees in the office and nearly 50 part-time transcribers who work from their homes.

Dollar Stretcher

Form a purchasing group with other business support services to buy large quantities of supplies so you can take advantage of bulk pricing.

No matter how small or large your company is, it's critical that you not neglect the administrative side. It won't do you much good if you do the work but never get around to sending out the invoices so you can get paid. Poorly maintained records can get you into trouble with the IRS and other government agencies. And if you aren't marketing on a regular basis, your business will eventually dry up.

Running a business support service takes a lot of energy. It helps if you enjoy people but are also able to work alone or in small groups. You'll need to be able to juggle several projects at the same time, and always make each client feel as though he or she is the most important person to you.

Tracking Inventory

Your inventory will most likely be limited to the supplies you consume and provide to your clients, so inventory management will not be the same challenge it is for a retailer or a manufacturer. Even so, you need to keep track of what you buy and use, and what you have on hand.

Store supplies in a central location that is cool, dry, and away from strong, direct sunlight. Be sure to rotate your stock, using supplies in a first-in, first-out order.

Decide what inventory items will be billed back to your customers and what items you consider part of your cost of production. For example, you wouldn't likely bill back the cost of regular paper, but if you supply special stationery, envelopes, or labels, it's reasonable to charge your clients for those items. Make notes of what you use on the work order so you don't forget.

Keeping Time Records

Create a work order and file for each project as soon as it comes in the door. Make notes of the dates, the type of work that was done, who did the work, how long it took, and the billing rate that applies. You can use the form at the end of this chapter (see page 24) or create your own. You can use the work order to create your invoice, or attach a copy of it to your invoice.

Homebased entrepreneur Rachelle Y. in Perrysburg, Ohio, says a work order can be especially useful when you are doing a variety of smaller projects for a client, and the person who actually pays the bills is not the person who requested the work. For example, you might have typed a few letters for the marketing department, but the bookkeeper may need to know more than that to process the invoice. "Remember, they can't actually see you do the work, so they want detailed information about what you did," she says.

Firing Clients

Sometimes you'll lose clients because they decide to use another service or do the

Bright Idea

Set up a system that helps keep the work flowing and the deadlines met. Some operators create a computerized spreadsheet; others simply mark their work on a project board or calendar. The key is to come up with a system that works for you so you can be sure not to overcommit yourself.

▲

The Times They Are a Changin'

As you work through the start-up process, you'll hear over and over about the importance of planning. And planning is indeed critical—you need to think ahead about what could happen and how you'll deal with it. But one of the most crucial aspects of planning is flexibility—no matter how thoroughly and carefully you plan, things will change.

One of the most obvious changes you'll deal with almost daily is technological advances. That will have an impact on your equipment and software, the services you provide, and your relationship with your clients. It's important that you pay attention to changes in technology that will affect both you and your clients.

You'll probably also see an evolution in your service package and client base. It may be because of technology, but it may also be because the market changes or your own preferences change. For example, Joann V. founded her Chicago business targeting the legal market and court reporters. Today, she does very little legal work; instead, her business is divided into two primary market groups: the insurance industry and audio and video production companies. Joann made the change because she found these markets more lucrative and more interesting than the legal market. She says it's easier to get people to work for you if you have fascinating work for them to do. This illustrates the wisdom of not getting so locked into your original plan that you fail to recognize opportunities when they appear.

work themselves, but sometimes you need to take the initiative to "lose" the client yourself—that is, you need to terminate your relationship for whatever reason.

It may be that the client is simply too demanding—everything is always a rush, they don't care that they are routinely asking you to stay up until all hours to get the work done, or they refuse to consider that you may have other clients who also need service. It may be that they don't pay on time, quibble over fees, or are just unpleasant to deal with for a variety of other reasons.

Whenever possible, you'll want to salvage the relationship, and you may be able to do that by communicating with the client about the issues that are creating problems. But when all else fails, and a client is causing you more trouble and misery than the money

> ⚠️ **Beware!**
> When clients are in a hurry for a project, they may try to pressure you into committing to an unrealistic deadline. Don't give in and promise something that isn't possible—you'll just have a problem later when you are unable to deliver.

they're paying you is worth, you should politely but firmly tell them you can't work for them anymore. If you feel comfortable referring them to another service, then by all means do so. But don't work for a client that is unprofitable or is making you unhappy or uncomfortable—there's too much business out there for you to invest your time that way.

Long-Term Planning

Beyond managing the day-to-day operations of your company, you need to think about the future. Even if all you want is to be a small, one-person shop, you need to have a plan to maintain your workload, income level, and client base.

"Even when I have all the work I want, I take the time to network," says Winter Park, Florida's Charlene D. "My business may be small, but it's a long-term commitment, and I want to protect it. And even though I don't need to make a lot of money, I want to be able to forecast my revenue with some degree of accuracy, and that takes thought and planning."

Cindy P. struggles with planning on a different scale. She wants her company to be larger, but there is no more space available in her current office building. One option she's considering is to move to another building with more space. Another option is to open a second office. "The problem is, I need someone to run it because I can't be in two places at one time, and I don't have anyone yet who can do that," she says. She's also exploring the idea of creating a franchise system that would help others get into the business.

The point is, no matter how busy you get in the present, you always need to have one eye on the future to assure the continuing success of your operation.

Work Order

ABC Secretarial Service

Name: _____

Company: _____

Street address: _____

City: _____ State: _____ Zip: _____

Phone number: _____ Fax number: _____

Driver's license number: _____

Social Security number: _____

Referred by (previous customer, Yellow Pages, etc.): _____

Estimate: _____

Date/time project dropped off: _____

Date/time project due: _____

Description of project: _____

_____

_____

_____

_____

Additional instructions: _____

_____

_____

*We will make every effort to locate and correct all errors prior to your review; however, **CLIENT** is responsible for final proof. Our responsibility is limited to providing you with original page(s) only and does not extend to duplicating charges. Therefore, proofread your project carefully **PRIOR** to duplication. Errors or omissions found thereafter are **CLIENT'S** responsibility.*

Your
Market

For any business to succeed, it must have customers—people or companies that buy the products or services it offers. Once you've decided what services you want to offer, you need to figure out who will likely buy them, and you do that with market research. It would be impossible to develop marketing strategies or an effective service menu without market research. This process provides you with data that will help you identify and reach particular market segments, and to solve or avoid marketing problems. A thorough market survey forms the foundation of any successful business.

The goal of market research is to identify your market, find out where it is and develop a strategy to communicate with prospective customers in a way that will convince them to buy from you. You have three broad markets for your business support service: the general public, small commercial and homebased businesses, and large corporations.

General Public

By "general public," we mean individual clients who are not businesses. The two largest segments of this market are people needing resume preparation and college students.

A job hunter creating or updating a resume may actually write the document and bring it to you for layout and printing; he or she may need you to assist in writing the content as well. Even when the unemployment rate is low, the resume market is significant because people don't have to be unemployed to need a resume.

Of course, many people have their own computers and can prepare their own resumes, but they may also realize the importance of having a professionally designed document, along with a well-written cover letter, for their job search.

There are thousands of higher-learning institutions in the United States with a collective enrollment of millions of students. Although many students prepare reports and papers themselves, enough of them will turn to a professional word-processing firm to make this market substantial.

Students working on particularly long papers, such as graduate theses or dissertations, are strong candidates for your service. And, of course, once they graduate, they may come back to you for assistance with their resumes.

In addition to students, the academic community may also be a source of business (think professors who need word processing, editing, and proofreading services for their books and articles).

If you are in a commercial location and want to offer photocopying, faxing, and shipping, you may also serve the general public with these services.

> ### Bright Idea
> If you are homebased with small children, consider looking for clients that are likely to be more family-friendly, such as schools and churches. Perrysburg, Ohio, homebased entrepreneur Rachelle Y. says those types of clients always seem to be more understanding of such things as bringing her children with her to pick up or deliver work than clients in other industries.

Small Businesses

Chances are, the majority of your clients will fall under this category. These are companies that require secretarial and administrative support but do not have the money, space, or need for a full-time employee. Or they may prefer to outsource specific tasks rather than invest in the talent and equipment necessary to get the job done right. And hiring temporary employees can be more costly than small businesses' needs demand.

As the number of small businesses continues to grow, so does your potential market. And the list of services they use is limited only by your imagination and personal preferences. As you develop relationships with small businesses, you'll be in a position to make suggestions that will increase the volume—or even expand the scope—of the work you do for them.

Typically, small businesses turn to business support service firms for word processing, faxing, photocopying, shipping, desktop publishing, mailing list management, dictation, and transcription.

Large Corporations

Even fairly large operations with full-time secretaries and administrative assistants may be candidates for your services. If a company has a temporary situation where they have more work than they can handle in-house, they may turn to you to pick up the overload. Or, like the small businesses mentioned earlier, they may prefer to outsource special projects rather than hire temporary workers. This is a smart move, because hiring temporary employees means training them and providing them with adequately equipped workstations. Sending the work to you eliminates that hassle and cost.

Large companies also use business support services when their own staff members are unavailable due to vacations or illness. They may not actually need a "tcmp," that is, someone to come in and be present in the office, but they may need someone who can handle all or part of the work of the absent staffer.

See the chart on page 28 for a list of potential client groups and the services they need.

Finding a Niche—or Niches

It's a good idea to select one or more key market groups to target. There are a number of valid reasons for choosing a well-defined market niche. By targeting a very specific market segment, you can tailor your service menu, marketing efforts, and customer service system to meet that segment's needs. You can refine your marketing efforts and gain a reputation within the industry for expertise in certain areas—which means you can charge more. Think about it: In the medical field, who earns more—

▲

Your Potential Market: Who Needs What?

To say that there is a tremendous demand for business support services is one thing, but when it gets down to the nitty-gritty of planning your business and targeting your market, you need more specifics. Here is a list that is representative (but by no means complete!) of typical client groups and the types of services they use:

Architects	Word processing documents and proposals
Associations	Newsletters, desktop publishing, mailing lists, word processing
Attorneys	Word processing, transcription, briefs, template design, form design, articles for various publications, database design and maintenance, newsletters
Churches, synagogues, and other religious organizations	Newsletters, bulletins, meeting minutes, fliers, news releases, welcome packages
Consultants	Word processing, transcription, proposals, correspondence
Copy shops	Desktop publishing, graphic design
Corporations (large)	Manuals, transcription, special projects
Graphic designers	Text input, proofreading
Individuals	Resumes, job applications, college and graduate school applications, computer training
Insurance companies,	Transcription, database management, proposals, brokerages, agencies, and word processing related businesses
Market research companies	Focus group and interview transcription
Physicians and medical offices	Medical transcription
Politicians/political campaigns	Desktop publishing, newsletters, fliers
Professors	Transcription, articles
Real estate brokers/agencies	Database management, mailing lists, newsletters, fliers
Sales representatives	Correspondence, mailing list management, reports, newsletters, fliers
Small businesses (in any industry)	Word processing, correspondence, general administrative support, billing, newsletters, scanning, training
Students	Word processing papers, proofreading and editing dissertations and other documents, entrance and scholarship applications, theses, transcription
Video production companies	Transcription
Writers (business, medical, technical, etc.)	Interview transcription, research, word processing

A Suite Market

An executive suite operation—where tenants rent office space and share common needs, such as a reception area and receptionist, copy machine, fax machine, and other equipment—can be the perfect niche for your business support service company. There are three ways to establish service in an executive suite.

1. The most common way is to actually start an executive suite company by leasing a sizable space in an office building, and then subleasing space to clients, providing them a package deal of both office space and administrative support services. Your clients' monthly rental fee would cover their office space and basic services, such as receptionist and telephone answering, and you can negotiate fees for additional services.

2. Commercial real estate developers sometimes recognize the need to provide more than just space to tenants—particularly small, growing companies. They might hire a business support service company to act as an executive suite management company, managing the property and providing office support services to the tenants.

3. You might consider entering into a joint venture agreement with a real estate developer to provide office support for tenants in a commercial building. In this sort of arrangement, your autonomy and profit potential would be greater than with the second option, but so will the degree of risk you take.

a family practitioner or a neurosurgeon? The neurosurgeon, naturally, because he's a specialist, and what he does requires greater skill. Some market niches you might consider include:

*   *Other business support services.* Let existing business owners know you're available for overflow or to work on a contract basis. Expect to have to sign confidentiality and noncompete agreements, but be sure any such contract limits you to only being prevented from marketing directly to the service's clients whose work you actually do. You might have to discount your rates to allow them to make a profit, but your marketing and sales costs will be minimal, which offsets the discount; however, be sure you are compensated for rush jobs.

In her early business days, Rachelle Y. in Perrysburg, Ohio, found marketing to other secretarial services an easy way to jump-start her own operation. "I contacted them and said I was working from home, and if they had overload, they could call me," she says. One thing she failed to do, which she realizes in retrospect, was to ask for a premium rate for rush jobs, or jobs that required her to work at night or on weekends to complete. "If I had asked for it, I think they would have paid it, because nobody in their office was either willing or able to do the work within the deadline," she says.

- *Specific professions or industries.* If you have expertise in a specific field, you may target your service to that field. Two of the most common are the legal and medical fields, particularly transcribing for these groups, because you'll need to be familiar with a long list of special terms and formatting requirements. Or you may want to target professional salespeople, such as manufacturers' reps, who work from their homes and need occasional administrative support. Chicago's Joann V. focuses on the insurance industry, and Cindy P. in Irvine, California, targets the legal field.

- *Geographic areas.* If you are in a densely populated area, perhaps an office center or a light industrial park, you may want to choose your market by geography. Determine your parameters, and then market to the companies within your service area, emphasizing the convenience of using your service.

- *Academic.* If you're near a college or university, you can serve a number of academic-related niches, including students, instructors, and even administrators.

Use the worksheet on page 31 to help determine if you've clearly defined your niche.

Understanding the Competition

One of the most basic elements of effective marketing is differentiating yourself from the competition. One marketing consultant calls it "eliminating the competition," because if you set yourself apart by doing something no one else does, then you essentially have no competition. However, before you can differentiate yourself, you first need to understand who your competitors are and why your clients might use them.

The easiest way to find your competitors is to browse through the Yellow Pages. Look under a variety of categories, including "Business Support Services," "Secretarial Services," "Desktop Publishing," "Typing Services," "Resume Services," "Notaries—Public," "Telephone Answering Services," and any other category that might cover a service you intend to offer.

For the most part, the operators we talked with have friendly relationships with their competitors. This is partly because few business support services are identical, and operators frequently turn to one another for

> **Tip...**
>
> ## Smart Tip
> Keep geography in mind as you develop your market. Though some business support services are so specialized that they have clients across the country, most serve a fairly limited geographical radius. Irvine, California, entrepreneur Cindy P., for example, says the bulk of her business is within a three- to five-mile radius of her office.

Market Niche Worksheet

How well have you defined your market niche? How comfortably and clearly you answer the following questions will tell you.

○ Who are my clients? _____

_____

_____

○ What services do they need? _____

_____

_____

○ Where are they located? _____

_____

_____

○ How many hours each month will I be able to bill? _____

_____

_____

○ What can I expect to earn per billable hour? _____

_____

_____

○ How will I communicate with my prospective clients? _____

_____

_____

_____

○ Will this market niche generate sufficient revenue for me to reach my income and profitability goals? _____

_____

_____

_____

_____

▲

Bright Idea

Building owners and managers are a great source of marketing information and referrals. They know their tenants and are in a position to give you valuable information that will help you, or to even make referrals. Making these alliances is well worth the time and effort.

referrals and assistance with work overloads. Call your competitors, ask to speak to the owner and introduce yourself. Tell them you're starting a new business and you want to find out what they do so you can refer clients if you get requests for services you don't offer. You might also let them know you're available to work as a subcontractor if they need you.

The easiest way to set yourself apart from the competition and build a strong, loyal client base is to offer top-notch, accurate, on-time service at reasonable rates. You don't have to be the cheapest service in town, but you do have to do quality work and deliver by your clients' deadlines.

Are You on a Mission?

At any given moment, most business support service owners have a very clear understanding of the mission of their company. It may not be written down, but they know what they are doing, how and where it's being done, and who their customers are. Most of the operators we talked with didn't have a formal written mission statement, but they could clearly and concisely articulate their mission when asked.

If you're a solo operator and want to stay small, it's probably enough for you to keep your mission statement in your head. But if you have employees and want to eventually become a large company, it will help if you are guided by a written mission statement that can be easily communicated to others.

"A mission statement defines what an organization is, why it exists, its reason for being," says Gerald Graham, dean of the W. Frank Barton School of Business at Wichita State University in Kansas. "Writing it down and communicating it to others creates a sense of commonality and a more coherent approach to what you're trying to do."

According to Graham, at a minimum your mission statement should define who your primary customers are; identify the products and services you produce; and describe the geographical location in which you operate. For example, your mission statement might read "Our mission is to provide small and midsize businesses in the Atlanta area with quality administrative support, including word processing, desktop publishing, and other computer-related services, done accurately and delivered on time at a reasonable price."

A mission statement should be short—usually just one sentence and certainly no more than two. A good idea is to cap it at 100 words. Graham says it is more important to adequately communicate the mission statement to employees than to customers.

"Sometimes an organization will try to use a mission statement primarily for promotion and then, as an aside, use it to help the employees identify what business they're in," he says. "That doesn't work very well. The most effective mission statements are developed strictly for internal communication and discussion, and then if something promotional comes out of it, fine." In other words, your mission statement doesn't have to be clever or catchy—just accurate.

And although your mission statement may never win an advertising or creativity award, it can still be a very effective customer relations tool. One idea is to print your mission statement on a poster-sized panel, have every employee sign it, and hang it in a prominent place so customers can see it. You can even include it on your brochures and invoices.

Before you write your mission statement, answer the questions on page 34. Then get to work.

Mission Statement Worksheet

To develop an effective mission statement, ask yourself these questions:

○ Who are my clients? _____

_____

○ Why does my company exist? Who do we serve? What is our purpose?

_____

_____

_____

○ What are our strengths, weaknesses, opportunities, and threats?

_____

_____

○ Considering the above, along with our expertise and resources, what business should we be in?

_____

_____

_____

○ What is important to us? What do we stand for?

_____

_____

_____

Now that you've answered those questions, you are ready to write your own mission statement. Use the area below.

_____

_____

_____

_____

_____

_____

5

Business
Structure

There's a lot more to starting a business support service than having a computer and being able to type. This chapter will discuss the various issues you need to consider when you're setting up.

Whether your goal is a part-time homebased business to supplement the family income or a full-time commercial company with employees and tremendous income and growth potential, you need to start with a written business plan. This helps you think through what you're doing, see your strengths and weaknesses, and figure out a way to overcome challenges on paper before you actually have to face them in real life. Writing a business plan is not an unpleasant but necessary chore; it's creating the foundation and setting the vision of your company.

Naming Your Company

Your company name can be an important marketing tool. A well-chosen name can work very hard for you; an ineffective name means you have to work much harder at marketing your firm and letting people know what you have to offer.

Regardless of what type of business you're in, your company name should very clearly identify what you do in a way that will appeal to your target market. It should be short, catchy, and memorable. It should also be easy to pronounce and spell—people who can't say your company name may use you, but they won't refer you to anyone else.

Many business support service owners simply use their own name and the primary service they provide, such as Voss Transcriptions Inc. A similar approach is to use some sort of regional or other descriptive designation, plus the primary service category offered, as one of the entrepreneurs we interviewed did. The company the entrepreneur bought used the previous owner's first name as its name, so the entrepreneur promptly renamed it Orange Coast Secretarial Service. "I actually wanted the name 'Orange County Secretarial Service,' but it was taken, so I went to Orange Coast," says the entrepreneur. "I wanted something that would sound like a larger company, even though it was just me at the time. But I wanted the appearance of something more than just a woman sitting there typing letters."

You might want to get clever. Consider WordCare, the name of another entrepreneur's company. The entrepreneur and his wife made a list of words related to the services they wanted to offer (word processing, office support, resumes, desktop publishing) and then began playing with various combinations until the came up with one they liked. "This one just fit, and I like the name," the entrepreneur says. "The only thing I don't like about it is that I'm at the bottom of the list in the Yellow Pages, but we figured it was a good enough name that it was worth it. And we've gotten good feedback on the name." Another entrepreneur's company

> **Bright Idea**
>
> When naming your company, consider creating a word that doesn't exist—that's what companies like Exxon and Kodak did. Just be sure the syllables blend to make an ear-appealing sound and that the name is simple enough for people to remember. Also, check to make sure you haven't inadvertently come up with a name that means (or even implies) something negative in another language.

name, Office Assistant Secretarial Service, was developed by a marketing company that also helped the entrepreneur put together a brochure and marketing package.

You may decide that your business doesn't even need a name. One of the entrepreneurs we spoke with works essentially as an independent contractor under her own name and doesn't use a business name. "It's easier that way," she says.

Take a systematic approach to naming your company. Once you've decided on two or three possibilities, take the following steps.

- *Check the name for effectiveness and functionality.* Does it quickly and easily convey what you do? Is it easy to say and spell? Is it memorable in a positive way? Ask several of your friends and associates to serve as a focus group to help you evaluate the name's impact.

- *Search for potential conflicts in your local market.* Find out if any other local or regional business serving your market area has a name so similar that yours might confuse the public.

- *Check for legal availability.* Exactly how you do this depends on the legal structure you choose. Typically, sole proprietorships and partnerships operating under a name other than that of the owner(s) are required by the county, city, or state to register their fictitious name. Even if it's not required, it's a good idea, because that means no one else can use that name. Your bank or local newspaper may be able to help you file for a fictitious name. Corporations usually operate under their corporate name. In either case, you need to check with the appropriate regulatory agency to be sure the name you choose is available.

- *Check for use on the World Wide Web.* If someone else is already using your name as a domain on the World Wide Web, consider coming up with something else. Even if you have no intention of developing a Web site of your own, the use could be confusing to your customers.

- *Check to see if the name conflicts with any name listed on your state's trademark register.* Your state Department of Commerce can either help you or direct you to the correct agency. You should also check with the trademark register maintained by the U.S. Patent and Trademark Office (PTO).

Once the name you've chosen passes these tests, you need to protect it by registering it with the appropriate state agency; again, your state Department of Commerce can help you. Though most business support services are local operations, if you expect to be doing business on a national level, you should also register the name with the PTO.

Legal Structure

One of the first decisions you'll need to make about your new business is the legal structure of your company. This is an important decision, and it can affect your financial liability, the amount of taxes you pay, the degree of ultimate control you have over the company, as well as your ability to raise money, attract investors, and ultimately sell the business. However, legal structure shouldn't be confused with operating structure. Attorney Robert S. Bernstein, managing partner with Bernstein Bernstein Krawec & Wymard, P.C., explains the difference: "The legal structure is the ownership structure—who actually owns the company. The operating structure defines who makes management decisions and runs the company."

A sole proprietorship is owned by the proprietor; a partnership is owned by the partners; and a corporation is owned by the shareholders. Another business structure is the limited liability company (LLC), which combines the tax advantages of a sole proprietorship with the liability protection of a corporation. The rules on LLCs vary by state; check with your state's Department of Corporations for the latest requirements.

Sole proprietorships and partnerships can be operated however the owners choose. In a corporation, the shareholders typically elect directors, who in turn elect officers, who then employ other people to run and work in the company. But it's entirely possible for a corporation to have only one shareholder and to essentially function as a sole proprietorship. In any case, how you plan to operate the company should not be a major factor in your choice of legal structures.

So what goes into choosing a legal structure? The first point, says Bernstein, is who is actually making the decision on the legal structure. If you're starting the company by yourself, you don't need to take anyone else's preferences into consideration. "But if there are multiple people involved, you need to consider how you're going to relate to each other in the business," he says. "You also need to consider the issue of asset protection and limiting your liability in the event things don't go well."

> **If your target market is going to be other businesses, it might enhance your image if you incorporate.**

Something else to think about is your target customers and what their perception will be of your structure. While it's not necessarily true, Bernstein says, "There is a tendency to believe that the legal form of a business has some relationship to the sophistication of the owners, with the sole proprietor as the least sophisticated and the corporation as the most sophisticated." If your target market is going to be other businesses, it might enhance your image if you incorporate. Your image notwithstanding, the biggest advantage of forming a corporation is in the area of asset protection, which, says Bernstein, is the process of making sure that the assets which you don't want to put into the business don't stand liable for the business's debt. However, to take advantage of the protection a corporation offers, you must respect the corporation's identity. That means maintaining the corporation as a separate entity; keeping your corporate

Beware!
Find out what type of licenses and permits are required for your business while you're still in the planning stage. You may find out that you can't legally operate the business you're envisioning, so give yourself time to make adjustments to your strategy before you've spent a lot of time and money trying to move in an impossible direction.

and personal funds separate, even if you are the sole shareholder; and following your state's rules regarding holding annual meetings and other record-keeping requirements.

Is any one of these structures better than another? No. We found business support services operating as sole proprietors, partners, and corporations, and they made their choices based on what was best for their particular situation, which is what you should do. For example, Chicago's Joann V. worked for ten years as a sole proprietor, and then, on the advice of her attorney, incorporated in 1994 after winning a large contract. By contrast, Cindy P. in Irvine, California, still operates as a sole proprietor. "We've grown significantly every year since I've had the business, but my CPA says it's not going to help me to incorporate, and she has advised me to wait."

Do you need an attorney to set up a corporation or a partnership? Again, no. Bernstein says there are plenty of good do-it-yourself books and kits on the market, and most of the state agencies that oversee corporations have guidelines you can use. Even so, it's always a good idea to have a lawyer at least look over your documents before you file them, just to make sure they are complete and will allow you to truly function as you want to.

Finally, remember that your choice of legal structure is not an irrevocable decision, although if you're going to make a switch, it's easier to go from the simpler forms to the more sophisticated ones than the other way around. Bernstein says the typical pattern is to start as a sole proprietor, and then move up to a corporation as the business grows. But if you need the asset protection of a corporation from the beginning, start out that way. Says Bernstein, "If you're going to the trouble to start a business, decide on a structure and put it all together. It's worth the extra effort to make sure it's really going to work."

Licenses and Permits

Most cities and counties require business operators to obtain various licenses and permits to comply with local regulations. While you are still in the planning stages, check with your local planning and zoning department or city/county business license department to find out what licenses and permits you will need and how to obtain them. You may need some or all of the following:

- *Occupational license or permit.* This is typically required by the city (or county if you are not within an incorporated city) for just about every business operating within its jurisdiction. License fees are essentially a tax, and the rates vary widely, based

▲

on the location and type of business. As part of the application process, the licensing bureau will check to make sure there are no zoning restrictions prohibiting you from operating.

- *Fire department permit.* If your business is open to the public, you may be required to have a permit from the local fire department.

- *Sign permit.* Many cities and suburbs have sign ordinances that restrict the size, location, and sometimes the lighting and type of sign you can use in front of your business. Landlords may also impose their own restrictions. Most residential areas forbid signs altogether. To avoid costly mistakes, check regulations and secure the written approval of your landlord before you invest in a sign.

- *State licenses.* Many states require persons engaged in certain occupations to hold licenses or occupational permits. Often, these people must pass state examinations before they can conduct business. States commonly require licensing for auto mechanics, plumbers, electricians, building contractors, collection agents, insurance agents, real estate brokers, repossessors, and personal service providers such as doctors, nurses, barbers, cosmetologists, etc. It is unlikely that you'll need a state license to operate your business support service, but it's a good idea to check with your state's occupation licensing entity to be sure.

Business Insurance

It takes a lot to start a business—even a small one—so protect your investment with adequate insurance. If you are homebased, don't assume your homeowners' or renters'

Just the Tax, Ma'am

Laws regarding the collection and remittance of sales tax vary by state, so you need to check with your state's Department of Revenue to see what you're required to do. Many states treat products and services differently when it comes to sales tax; for example, you may not be required to charge tax on your word-processing fees, but you might have to collect sales tax on labels you print for your customers.

Typically, you'll be required to file your state sales tax return quarterly, but this varies by state and can often be negotiated based on your volume. If you are in a state that does not tax services and your taxable sales are likely to be limited to a very small amount of office supplies, you may even be allowed to file annually.

Whatever you do, don't be careless about sales tax. Failing to properly collect and remit sales tax is a serious crime with very unpleasant consequences.

Smart Tip

When you purchase insurance on your equipment and inventory, ask what documentation the insurance company requires before you have to file a claim. That way, you'll be sure to maintain appropriate records, and the claims process will be easier if it is ever necessary.

policy covers your business equipment; chances are, it doesn't. If you're located in a commercial facility, be prepared for your landlord to require proof of certain levels of liability insurance when you sign the lease. And in either case, you need coverage for your equipment, supplies, clients' materials, and other valuables.

A smart approach to insurance is to find an agent who works with other professional services businesses. The agent should be willing to help you analyze your needs, evaluate the risks you're willing to accept, and the risks you need to insure against, and work with you to keep your insurance costs down.

Typically, homebased business support services will want to make sure their equipment and supplies are insured against theft and damage by a covered peril, such as fire or flood, and that they have some liability protection if someone (either a customer or an employee) is injured on their property. In most cases, one of the new insurance products designed for homebased businesses will provide sufficient coverage. Also, if you use your vehicle for business, be sure it is adequately covered.

If you opt for a commercial location, your landlord will probably require certain levels of general liability coverage as part of the terms of your lease. You'll also want to cover your supplies, equipment, and fixtures. Once your business is up and running, consider business interruption insurance to replace lost revenue and cover related costs if you are ever unable to operate due to covered circumstances.

Although it's not extremely common in the business support service industry, you may have clients who want to see a certificate of insurance or who want to be listed as an insured on your liability coverage. Your insurance agent should be able to help you with this paperwork.

The insurance industry is responding to the special needs of small businesses by developing affordable products that provide coverage on equipment, liability, and even loss of income. Bill P. in Iowa City, Iowa, says his small-business package gives him the coverage he needs for peace of mind at a nominal fee.

Professional Services

As a business owner, you may be the boss, but you can't be expected to know everything. You'll occasionally need to turn to professionals for information and assistance. It's a good idea to establish a relationship with these professionals before you get into a crisis situation.

To shop for a professional service provider, ask your friends and associates for recommendations. You might also check with your local chamber of commerce or trade

▲

association for referrals. Find someone who understands your industry and specific business and appears eager to work with you. Check them out with the Better Business Bureau and the appropriate state licensing agency before committing yourself.

As a business support service owner, the professional service providers you're likely to need include:

Smart Tip

Sit down with your insurance agent every year and review your insurance needs. As your company grows, they are sure to change. Also, insurance companies are always developing new products to meet the needs of the growing small-business market, and it's possible one of these new policies is appropriate for you.

- *Attorney.* You need a lawyer who practices in the area of business law, is honest, and appreciates your patronage. In most parts of the United States, there are many lawyers willing to compete fiercely for the privilege of serving you. Interview several and choose one you feel comfortable with. Be sure to clarify the fee schedule ahead of time, and get your agreement in writing. Keep in mind that good commercial lawyers don't come cheap; if you want good advice, you must be willing to pay for it. Your attorney should review all contracts, leases, letters of intent, and other legal documents before you sign them. He or she can also help you with collecting bad debts and establishing personnel policies and procedures. Of course, if you are unsure of the legal ramifications of any situation, call your attorney immediately.

- *Accountant.* Among your outside advisors, your accountant is likely to have the greatest impact on the success or failure of your business. If you are forming a corporation, your accountant should counsel you on tax issues during start-up. On an ongoing basis, your accountant can help you organize the statistical data concerning your business, assist in charting future actions based on past performance, and advise you on your overall financial strategy regarding purchasing, capital investment, and other matters related to your business goals. A good accountant will also serve as a tax advisor, making sure you are in compliance with all applicable regulations and that you don't overpay any taxes.

- *Insurance agent.* A good independent insurance agent can assist with all aspects of your business insurance, from general liability to employee benefits, and probably even handle your personal lines, as well. Look for an agent who works with a wide range of insurers and understands your particular business. This agent should be willing to explain the details of various types of coverage, consult with you to determine the best coverage, help you understand the degree of risk you are taking, work with you in developing risk-reduction programs, and assist in expediting any claims.

Cover Me

Errors and omissions (E&O) insurance protects you in the event you make a mistake that causes damage to a client. Whether or not you need this particular coverage depends on the type of work you're doing.

For the most part, says Lynette M. Smith, executive director of the Association of Business Support Services International Inc., the business support service industry falls under the trade custom of the printing industry (final proofreading is the responsibility of the client, and your liability is limited to providing a corrected draft of the project, and not to any subsequent printing, postage, or loss-of-business aspects of the situation, such as an inaccurate phone number or date). Even so, you should remind your clients of this custom and urge them to proofread the work carefully before using it in any way. It's also a good idea to have clients sign and date their approval of drafts, particularly when the project is critical or a mistake could be costly.

"Because of this trade custom, the need for errors and omissions insurance may be considered necessary only for medical transcription and perhaps legal transcription," says Smith. "I recommend those two areas because these clients—doctors and attorneys—are the ones most likely to be sued capriciously, and it's hard for the outside service provider to stay out of the litigious loop once it begins. Having E&O insurance may help reduce financial and other inconveniences during litigation."

E&O insurance may also be something to consider if you offer services outside what is considered standard business support services (word processing, desktop publishing, database management, etc.), where your client has the opportunity to check and approve the final product. If you offer any type of consulting, research services, Web site design, or other professional service, you may want to protect yourself with E&O coverage.

- *Banker.* You need a business bank account and a relationship with a banker. Don't just choose the bank you've always done your personal banking with; it may not be the best bank for your business. Interview several bankers before making a decision on where to place your business. Once your account is opened, maintain a relationship with the banker. Periodically sit down and review your accounts and the services you use to make sure you are getting the package most appropriate for your situation. Ask for advice if you have financial questions or problems. When you need a loan or a bank reference to provide to creditors, the relationship you've established will work in your favor.

- *Consultants.* The consulting industry is booming, and for good reason. Consultants can provide valuable, objective input on all aspects of your business. Consider hiring a business consultant to evaluate your business plan or a marketing consultant to assist you in that area. When you are ready to hire employees, a human resources consultant may help you avoid some costly mistakes. Consulting fees vary widely, depending on the individual's

> ### Smart Tip
> Not all attorneys are created equal, and you may need more than one. For example, the lawyer who can best guide you in contract negotiations may not be the most effective counsel when it comes to employment issues. Ask about areas of expertise and specialization before retaining a lawyer.

experience, location, and field of expertise. If you can't afford to hire a consultant, consider contacting the business school at the nearest college or university and hiring an MBA student to help you.

- *Computer expert.* Your computer is your most valuable physical asset, so if you don't know much about computers, find someone to help you select a system and the appropriate software, and who will be available to help you maintain, trouble-shoot, and expand your system as you need it.

Most of the business owners we talked with have ongoing relationships with accountants and know of an attorney they can call on if they need one. They also have other advisors. For example, Joann V.'s sister owns an insurance agency, so Joann turns to her for advice on insurance issues and general business management issues.

Creating Your Own Advisory Board

Not even the president of the United States is expected to know everything. That's why he surrounds himself with advisors—experts in particular areas who provide knowledge and information to help him make decisions. Savvy small-business owners use a similar strategy.

You can assemble a team of volunteer advisors to meet with you periodically to offer advice and direction. Because this isn't an official or legal entity, you have a great deal of latitude in how you set it up. Advisory boards can be structured to help with the direct operation of your company and to keep you informed on various business, legal, and financial trends that may affect you. Use these tips to set up your advisory board:

- *Structure a board that meets your needs.* Generally, you'll want a legal advisor, an accountant, a marketing expert, a human resources person, and perhaps a financial advisor. You may also want successful entrepreneurs from other industries who understand the basics of business and will view your operation with a fresh eye.

- *Ask the most successful people you can find, even if you don't know them well.* You'll be surprised at how willing people are to help another business succeed.

- *Be clear about what you are trying to do.* Let your prospective advisors know what your goals are and that you don't expect them to take on an active management role or to assume any liability for your company or for the advice they offer.

- *Don't worry about compensation.* Advisory board members are rarely compensated with more than lunch or dinner. Of course, if a member of your board provides a direct service—for example, if an attorney reviews a contract or an accountant prepares a financial statement—then they should be paid at their normal rate. But that's not part of their job as an advisory board member. Keep in mind that, even though you don't write them a check, your advisory board members will likely benefit in a variety of tangible and nontangible ways. Being on your board will expose them to ideas and perspectives they may not otherwise see, and will also expand their own network.

- *Consider the group dynamics when holding meetings.* You may want to meet with all the members together, or in small groups of one or two. It all depends on how they relate to each other and what you need to accomplish.

- *Ask for honesty, and don't be offended when you get it.* Your pride might be hurt when someone points out something you're doing wrong, but the awareness will be beneficial in the long run.

- *Learn from failure as well as success.* Encourage board members to tell you about their mistakes so you can avoid making them.

- *Respect the contribution your board members are making.* Let them know you appreciate how busy they are, and don't abuse or waste their time.

- *Make it fun.* You are, after all, asking these people to donate their time, so create a pleasant atmosphere.

- *Listen to every piece of advice.* Stop talking and listen. You don't have to follow every piece of advice, but you need to hear it.

- *Provide feedback to the board.* Good or bad, let the board know what you did and what the results were.

Beware!

Never just sign a delivery receipt for packages. Even though you'll get to know your regular driver, always count the packages and do a quick visual inspection for external signs of damage.

Shipping and Receiving

Unless you're going to offer shipping and receiving as a service to your clients, you aren't likely to have to deal with this aspect of business much.

If you decide to offer shipping and receiving, chances are most of your shipments will be small enough to be handled by UPS (United Parcel Service), Federal Express, Airborne, the United States Postal Service

(USPS), and similar companies. Contact the customer service departments of the package and courier companies serving your area to set up an account so they will bill you, and to arrange for regular pickups if you need them. If your clients are shipping large volumes of material, it's likely they'll have their own staff and facilities to handle it.

Your clients may select the carrier they want you to use, or they may leave the choice up to you. If you have chosen the carrier, make sure the freight company has insurance to cover accidents or losses because if the carrier makes a mistake, is late with a delivery, or loses or damages a package, it could have a negative impact on your relationship with your customers. Choose your freight companies carefully and demand that they perform up to your high standards.

Dollar Stretcher

When it comes to freight services, don't pay for more than you need. Most overnight companies offer two or three levels of next-day service—early morning, before noon, and afternoon. The earlier the guaranteed delivery, the higher the cost. If the next afternoon will meet your customer's needs, don't pay for morning delivery. And if the carrier misses its delivery commitment, insist that it honor its guarantee by refunding the charges.

Start-Up
Economics

One of the most appealing aspects of the business support service industry is its relatively low start-up costs. If you have a decent credit rating, you can be ready to start serving clients with virtually no cash out of pocket—although you'll certainly be on firmer ground if you have some start-up capital. Chapter 9 discusses the specific equipment you'll need, along with price ranges. But whether all you have is a credit card or you've got a nice fat savings account ready to invest, opening your doors is only part of the financial picture.

The issue of money has two sides: How much do you need to start and operate, and how much can you expect to take in? Doing this analysis is often extremely difficult for small-business owners who would rather be in the trenches getting the work done than bound to a desk dealing with tiresome numbers.

Most of the business support service entrepreneurs we talked with used their own personal savings and equipment they already owned to start their businesses. Because the start-up costs are relatively low, you'll find traditional

Photo© PhotoDisc Inc.

financing difficult to obtain—banks and other lenders would much rather lend amounts much larger than you'll need and are likely to be able to qualify for.

Many operators start their businesses on the side while working full-time jobs, so their personal living expenses are covered. But if you plan to plunge into your new business full time from the start, be sure you have enough cash on hand to cover your expenses until the revenue starts coming in. At a minimum, you should have the equivalent of three months' expenses in a savings account to tap if you need it; you'll probably sleep better if you have six to 12 months of expenses socked away.

As you're putting together your financial plan, consider these sources of start-up funds:

- *Your own resources.* Do a thorough inventory of your assets. People generally have more assets than they immediately realize. This could include savings accounts, equity in real estate, retirement accounts, vehicles, recreation equipment, collections, and other investments. You may opt to sell assets for cash or use them as collateral for a loan. Take a look, too, at your personal line of credit; most of the equipment you'll need is available through retail stores that accept credit cards.

- *Friends and family.* The logical next step after gathering your own resources is to approach your friends and relatives who believe in you and want to help you succeed. Be cautious with these arrangements; no matter how close you are, present yourself professionally, put everything in writing, and be sure the individuals you approach can afford to take the risk of investing in your business.

- *Partners.* Though most business support services are owned by just one person, you may want to consider using the "strength in numbers" principle and look around for someone who may want to team up with you in your venture. You may choose someone who has financial resources and wants to work side-by-side with you in the business. Or you may find someone who has money to invest but no interest in doing the actual work. Be sure to create a written partnership agreement that clearly defines your respective responsibilities and obligations.

- *Government programs.* Take advantage of the abundance of local, state, and federal programs designed to support small businesses. Make your first stop the U.S. Small Business Administration; then investigate various other programs. Women, minorities, and veterans should check out niche financing possibilities designed to help these groups get into business. The business section of your local library is a good place to begin your research.

How Much Do You Need?

So what do you need in the way of cash and available credit to open your doors? Depending on what you already own, the services you want to offer and whether you'll be homebased or in a commercial location, that number could range from a few hundred to thousands of dollars.

Charlene D. in Winter Park, Florida, decided to invest in a new computer and printer and says she spent about $3,500 on equipment and supplies to get started. Perrysburg, Ohio's Rachelle Y. used her old 486 PC to develop her business plan and brochure but decided to purchase a new system before she actually began her operation. "I wanted to be able to offer everything I could," she says. "In this field, your computer is your best friend. So I bought a new computer and printer, paper, and some other odds and ends. I probably spent between $3,000 and $4,000 on start-up."

In Iowa City, Iowa, Bill P. and his wife used credit to buy the company's first computer and printer and managed to get up and running with a cash outlay of less than $1,000. Because he was a student at the time, he bought and financed his computer at a

Beware!

Most of the equipment you need can be purchased at a retail store and charged on a credit card—but too much debt can doom your business before it gets off the ground. Only use your credit cards for items that will contribute to revenue generation, and have a repayment plan in place before you buy.

discount (total cost of about $2,500) through the university; most of the initial cash was spent on marketing.

Irvine, California's Cindy P. paid $10,000 to buy an existing business; that fee included the client list and the lease on the office, but no furniture or equipment. She spent another $4,000 on initial equipment purchases and has added more over the years.

Joann V. in Chicago started her business before the days of PCs. "Originally, all I needed was a typewriter," she says. "I bought an electronic typewriter for $500 and some paper, and someone loaned me a transcription unit. That was it—that was all I needed to start." In Edmond, Oklahoma, Janet S. says that because she already owned a com-

Beware!

If you use subcontractors, be sure the difference between what you pay them and what you're charging your client is great enough so your profit will be worthwhile. When you subcontract to other business support services, you may find them willing to offer a discount—to essentially "wholesale" their services to you, and you "retail" the finished work to the client. In any case, if you can't make a profit, subcontracting is a waste of time.

puter, printer, and answering machine, her start-up costs were "virtually zero."

As you consider your own situation, don't pull a start-up number out of the air; use your business plan to calculate how much you will need to start your ideal operation, and then figure out how much you have. If you have all the cash you need, you are very fortunate. If you don't, you need to start playing with the numbers and start deciding what you can do without.

The chart on the following page will serve as a guide for creating a start-up budget for your business. Prices are estimated ranges and will vary depending on features, sources, and whether they are new or used. Ranges beginning with $0 are either optional or items you're likely to already own and therefore don't need to purchase.

Pricing Your Services

You have a number of options when it comes to deciding on your approach to pricing. Some operators simply call around, find out what other companies are charging and set their prices in that range. Others decide what they want to earn and set their prices based on that without regard to how it relates to the competition. Then there's the issue of pricing by the project, the page, or the hour.

The best approach is a multifaceted one that considers the skill level of the work, your profit goals, and the market. You need to set up a system that gives you a structure to work within so you can quote consistent, reasonable and fair rates.

Multiple Hourly Rates

If you're going to charge by the hour, consider that different rates should apply depending on the complexity of the service and skill level required. For example, Cindy P.'s hourly rate ranges from $28 for straight word processing up to $40 for complex

Start-Up Budget Guide

Item	Price Range
Computer system (including printer)	$2,000–4,500
Typewriter	$0–500
Fax machine	$100–600
Accounting/billing software	$75–300
Other software	$0–2,000
Phone system	$0–500
Answering machine	$0–150
Uninterruptible power supply	$90–200
Zip drive	$100–150
Tape transcription machine	$150–300
Surge protector	$30–150
Calculator	$0–100
Copier	$200–500
Desk and chair	$0–1,000
Printer stand	$50–150
File cabinet(s)	$50–500
Bookcase(s)	$30–150
Computer/copier paper	$0–25
Stationery (business cards, letterhead, envelopes)	$75–400
Address stamp	$5–25
Extra printer cartridge	$75–150
Extra fax cartridge	$30–70
Miscellaneous office supplies	$0–200

desktop publishing. The Association of Business Support Services International (ABSSI) suggests a structure similar to the following:

- *Level 1 (lowest hourly rate).* Basic word processing, routine clerical services, simple proofreading
- *Level 2.* Enhanced word processing, copy editing, proofreading, basic spreadsheet design, Internet research
- *Level 3.* Desktop publishing, spreadsheet design, simple Web page design, simple Web page maintenance
- *Level 4.* Graphic design, writing (academic, business, resume, technical), Web page design, Web page maintenance
- *Level 5 (highest hourly rate).* Consulting, training

Note that the same basic task might fall into more than one pricing level, and you'll need to make a judgment call based on the particular project as to which rate to apply.

> **Bright Idea**
>
> Periodically check on what the competition is charging. How? Call and ask. Most will tell you—and though some won't, you'll still get enough to ensure your fees are competitive, but not significantly over or under where the general market is.

Estimating the Job

Many new business owners find estimating one of the most challenging things they do, but if you approach the process systematically, it's simple. You just need to determine an appropriate hourly rate, calculate the length of time the project should take, and do the math.

Regardless of the format you use to provide the quote (written or verbal), it's a good idea to make notes for yourself so you know what you quoted and how you

Bottom Dollar

Y ou may want to consider setting a minimum—either a dollar amount or an hourly figure—that you bill clients with very small jobs. This takes into consideration the reality that every job requires a certain amount of administrative time (setting up the project, billing, receiving, and processing the payment, etc.), regardless of how small or large the actual project is. So if you bill by the hour, for example, you might have a minimum charge of one hour, regardless of whether the work took you the full hour or just a few minutes. You can, of course, waive the minimum charge for regular clients who give you a substantial amount of work.

Hour Power

When the Association of Business Support Services International surveyed its members, it found that the range of hourly rates for the most popular services offered by respondents were:

Basic word processing	$7–40
Enhanced word processing	$7–50
Copy editing	$7–75
Database entry	$18–50
Transcription, general	$15–45
Consulting/training	$7–90
Spreadsheet design	$15–75
Desktop publishing	$7–75
Graphic design	$14–100
Web site design	$20–150
Internet research	$7–75

arrived at that figure. This will be necessary if the actual project turns out to be different from what the client described, or if the client questions the invoice later, even though they agreed to the quote. You may even want to create an estimate form that you can provide to the client and keep a copy in your own files. Use the estimate form on page 54 to help you get started.

Charlene D. bills by the hour, but she always gives her clients a high-end cap on the project. "I tell them what the hourly rate is, and also how much time I think the project will take," she says. "I want them to have a fair assessment of what it's going to cost them. You can't say 'It's so much an hour, but I don't know how many hours it will take.' If I overestimate the time, then they're happy because they get a bill that's smaller than they anticipated. If I underestimate, I call them as soon as I realize it and we talk about it and work something out." And that last issue brings up another important point about pricing: You need a clear picture of the entire project, and your price quote should include a description of what you understand the project to be in case there's a discrepancy later. "It's beneficial to everyone if the client is honest about the scope of the project from the very beginning," Charlene says.

Joann V. says many of her clients prefer a page rate, so she has rates for single-spaced and double-spaced pages. She also has an hourly rate. Janet S. charges by the

Estimate Form

Client name: _____

Contact: _____

Address (optional): _____

_____

_____

Phone: _____

Fax: _____

Project description: _____

_____

_____

_____

_____

Fee: $ _____ per hour (or) Total: $ _____

Possible additional services: _____

_____

_____

_____

_____

Fee for additional services: $ _____ per hour (or) Total: $ _____

Estimate provided to client on (date): _____

Price valid until (date): _____

page for college papers and resumes, and by the hour for businesses. She has a discounted rate for nonprofit organizations.

The Danger of Pricing Too Low

If the client says your quote is too high, consider taking away services to bring the price down—don't just lower the fee. Reducing your rates without any concession from the client says you didn't feel you were worth what you wanted to charge in the first place. Be sure to put the terms in writing so the client doesn't complain later.

Many new operators take the approach of undercutting existing services as a way to break into the market, but this strategy can backfire. When Cindy P. bought her business, she lowered her rates to attract business but quickly realized she'd made a mistake. "I was thinking that I needed clients, and if I lowered my rates, I'd get business. That's absolutely wrong," she says. "You need to be paid according to the level of knowledge and experience you have. Cutting rates only made me look like my service wasn't good and like I needed to lower my rates to compensate for lower quality so people would use me. You can't grow a business and make a profit that way."

Industry Production Standards

There is a move in the industry to set prices according to accepted standards rather than based on the actual time it takes someone to do a particular project. The concept makes sense for both the service provider and the client.

Consider this scenario: A client has 90 minutes of audiotape that needs to be transcribed and calls three different services for a quote. The first operator's keyboarding speed is relatively slow, and she is unfamiliar with the client's industry and terminology, so she estimates that it will take her 7.5 hours to complete the work. The second operator's keyboarding speed is faster, but she is also unfamiliar with the industry and expects to be slowed by terms she hasn't heard before, so she estimates 6.5 hours to complete the work. The third operator types even faster than the second and knows the industry and its jargon well, so she estimates 4.5 hours to transcribe the tape.

If all of these operators are charging at the same hourly rate, the first service would actually make substantially more money even though it doesn't have the skill level or experience as the other two. The third service would actually be penalized for being skilled and knowledgeable.

Using an industry standard to determine the project length and classify its complexity

Smart Tip

Using production standards to set prices speeds up your estimating process, makes your quotes consistent and provides you with a tool to measure productivity and profitability.

Tip...

55

protects clients from excessive time billing by slower service providers and rewards faster service providers for their efficiency—and all the while protects the client by assuring fair pricing.

The ABSSI has published the *Industry Production Standards Guide*, which lists how long a "model operator" should take to complete certain tasks, how tasks should be classified, and also includes time that may be billable (such as meeting with clients, picking up work, discussing work over the phone, etc.) that you may overlook.

> ## Bright Idea
>
> Do an annual rate review. Once a year, look at all the fees you charge, and check to make sure the rate is profitable, in line with the market, and fair and reasonable for the service provided. If necessary, make adjustments to your rate structure.

Cindy P. finds that using production standards for billing lets her charge consistent amounts that are fair to both her and her clients. "We bill by the hour based on 70 words per minute. We do a character count and see how much work they actually did, and that's how we bill," she explains. This way, the service doesn't make less money if the typist is fast (and Cindy has employees who type at 100 words per minute and better), and the client doesn't pay extra if the typist is slow or having an off day.

Your Business
Location

When it comes to the actual site of your business, you have two choices: homebased or a commercial location. A business support service company can be extremely successful in either venue; your decision will depend on your individual resources and goals.

As you consider the issue of location, keep a few things in mind. Depending on the specific services you offer and market you target, you may be dealing both with the general public, who will need access to your office, and with small-business owners and managers in larger corporations who may also want to visit your facility or have their employees or a messenger pick up and deliver work.

In any business, but especially in this one, a professional image is a critical element of success. Homebased operations are very accepted in today's business world (in fact, many customers prefer dealing with homebased suppliers because they have lower overhead and can therefore charge less), but you still need to present the appearance of being a serious business, even though you may choose to work from your house. And if you opt for a commercial location, be sure it is one that is compatible with your goals.

Many operators start from home with the goal of moving into commercial space as soon as they're established with a few clients, and this is an excellent strategy. Joann V. in Chicago worked at home for the first six months and then rented office space from a friend who had a secretarial service. "I paid her $150 a month, and I also had to sit at the front desk and be her receptionist, and if she had overflow, I helped her," Joann recalls. "It was a great deal. I couldn't have started any other way because rent in the Chicago area is pretty high." Today, she's in her own large office and is subleasing space to other small businesses.

In the mid-1990s, about half the members of the Association of Business Support Services International (ABSSI) were homebased; by the turn of the century, an estimated 70 percent were homebased, one-person operations. "Many of our previously office-based members are simplifying their lives by moving back to a residential location," says Lynette M. Smith, ABSSI's executive director. "They acknowledge that a homebased business is no longer the exception but the norm. In the perception of clients, there no longer is a stigma associated with being homebased."

While conceding that operating from home can make growth challenging, Smith says, "At home, one cannot expand through the traditional means of hiring employees. However, it is becoming more realistic to subcontract out work—especially transcription—to others, so there is still significant profit potential to be expected by replicating one's efforts in this way."

Homebased Operations

The major benefit of starting a homebased business is the fact that it significantly reduces the amount of start-up and initial operating capital you'll need. But there's more to consider than simply the upfront cash. You need to be conveniently located so your clients can get to you and/or you can get to them without wasting time traveling. Though some types of work won't require a great deal of ongoing interaction with the client, other types will. If you're doing desktop publishing, for example, your client may want to review proofs at several stages. Even if they're willing to come to you to do that,

Beware!

The typical suburban home is often not the best location in which to operate a business support service company. You will most likely be isolated from commercial districts, and parking will be limited. If this is your situation, be sure your market is compatible with your location.

they're not going to want to drive great distances. And if they expect you to bring the proofs to them, you don't want to have to spend a lot of unprofitable time in your car.

So the first thing you need to think about is whether or not your home is conveniently located in relation to your target market. In addition to actual proximity, consider accessibility. If clients will be coming to your office, you need to be located on or near a main street. Your neighborhood may be charming and your house perfect for a homebased business, but if your clients have to travel on a number of small side streets to reach you, they may abandon you for a more easy-to-reach provider. Along these lines, parking should be plentiful and easily available at no charge to your clients.

Next, think about your home itself. Do you have a separate room for an office, or will you have to work at the dining room table? Can you set up a comfortable workstation

Put Out the Welcome Mat?

A challenge for many homebased business owners is deciding where to meet with clients, particularly when they are strangers. Many business support service operators are not comfortable inviting strangers into their homes, especially if they are home alone or with small children, and this is a valid concern.

You don't need to express any fear or apprehension. Simply say "It's my policy to meet with clients either in their office or at a neutral place. Which do you prefer?"

The ideal solution is to meet at the client's office, but if this isn't practical or possible, a good alternative is to meet in a public place, such as a library, restaurant, or hotel lobby. If you must have your children with you, try a fast-food restaurant with a playground area where they can occupy themselves while you and your client discuss business.

If the client is pushy about wanting to come to your home even after you have indicated a preference for a public location, consider whether or not this is a client you would like to have. Your clients may not be a threat to your physical safety, but their disregard for your comfort level is a sign that they will probably be a difficult person to deal with.

with all the tools and equipment you'll need? Can you separate your work area from the rest of the house so you can have privacy when you're working and get away from "the office" when you're not?

Even if you are able to dedicate a room to your business, keep in mind that your clients may come to your home to drop off and pick up work or to review work in progress. This means that not only does your office need to appear professional, but the other areas of your home that clients may see should be neat and orderly and reflect the impression you want to create. Leading your clients through a living room cluttered with toys or past a kitchen with dirty dishes does not create a strong professional image. Keep pets and children out of the way when clients are in your office.

Commercial Locations

If you decide on a commercial location, your range of options is fairly broad, and your choice should be guided largely by the specific services you want to provide and the market you want to reach. Starting in a commercial location requires more initial cash than starting from home, but the business you can attract by having an office location can make up for this expense.

A good location for your business is an office building with other businesses (that may also be clients) or in an executive suite (again, the other tenants may become clients). Of course, don't restrict your marketing efforts to tenants in your building; reach out to other businesses in the area.

You may also want to consider a retail location, such as a shopping center. This would be appropriate if you are targeting students, individuals, and homebased business owners. It will give you some walk-in traffic for services such as photocopying and notarizing and may be more easily accessible for some of your clients than many commercial offices.

Regardless of the specific place, a commercial location gives you a degree of credibility that is hard to earn in a homebased office. You'll also have space to store the equipment and supplies you'll use in the course of your business, and create a setup that is more efficient and practical than what you might be able to do in a spare bedroom. You'll probably only need 200 to 400 square feet at first, and you should be able to find an office that size in a good location at a fairly reasonable price. Sharing office space with a noncompeting or complementary business to save money may also be an option.

Bright Idea

Consider any special market niches you plan to target when choosing your location. For example, if you intend to specialize in legal transcription, you'll want an office downtown near the courthouse, where most of the lawyers' offices are. If you plan to target students, you'll want to be near a college or university.

Smart Tip

Whether you are home-based or commercial-based, be sure your office has adequate electrical capacity. You'll need an ample supply of "clean" current without fluctuations that could damage your equipment. You'll also need plenty of outlets so you can safely plug in all your equipment—many older office buildings and homes are lacking in this area. Consult with an electrician or a representative from your local power company to make sure your office has the capacity to support your needs.

In addition to the building itself, consider your location within the building. A lobby office is ideal, because it gives your clients easy access while exposing you to everyone who enters the building. A location opposite the elevator doors can also give you fairly good exposure if a number of people make stops at your floor. But an office at the end of a hallway or in a place where no one passes will mean you have virtually no chance of attracting new business from passers-by.

Office Layout and Décor

A number of factors will influence how you arrange your office. Are you homebased or in a commercial location? Are you a one-person shop, or do you have employees, and, if so, how many? Exactly what services do you provide, and what type of equipment do you use?

Given all the variables involved, it's impossible to suggest an ideal, one-size-fits-all layout. But there are some points you need to consider.

If you're in a commercial location, it's a good idea to have a counter at the front of the office. When clients walk in, they can discuss their needs at the counter, where they can spread out any necessary documents. They can also drop off any materials you may need from them, such as letterhead, imprinted envelopes, or labels, etc. Use the counter to display your own marketing materials, policies, and other promotional items—but don't let it get too cluttered. The space under the counter can be used for storage.

If you offer photocopying or fax services, put these machines near the front counter so your clients can serve themselves but you can still keep an eye on them. Behind the counter, set up workstations for yourself and your employees.

While much of your consultation with clients can be done across a counter, if some clients will need to proofread documents, you should set up a space where they can do this without distractions. Ideally, this would be a small, enclosed room, but it could also be a desk or work table off to the side of your main office. If you are offering resume writing, consulting, and career coaching, you will need an enclosed, semisoundproofed area that allows privacy and confidentiality for your clients.

Your office décor should be businesslike, efficient, and attractive. You don't need to spend a lot of money on elegant furnishings, but you do need to make sure you create a favorable impression in your clients' minds. A good coat of paint will go a long way in brightening up your environment. Neutral shades such as beige or muted gray are good choices and will let you highlight your interior with bold graphics, posters, art prints, or bulletin boards. A few large plants will also add to the ambience, but be sure you maintain them. A healthy plant is not only attractive, but it also helps to maintain clean indoor air; a wilted, droopy plant with brown leaves may make your clients wonder just how well you'll do their work if you can't even manage to take care of a plant.

Desks and chairs should be attractive and functional but not luxurious. Invest in ergonomically sound chairs and equipment to preserve your health and productivity—and that of your employees. Be sure trash cans are emptied regularly and that the office is kept clean and dusted. Periodically take a look at your office through the eyes of a client who has never seen it before, and think about the impression it makes.

Human Resources

Though the majority of business support services are one-person operations, you may want a larger company. Or your goal may be to stay small, but you may need extra help once in a while. Whatever the case, it's a good idea for you to understand the human resources aspects of owning a business.

▲

The first step in formulating a comprehensive human resources program is to decide exactly what you want someone to do. The job description doesn't have to be as formal as one you might expect from a large corporation, but it needs to clearly outline the person's duties and responsibilities. It should also list any special skills or other required credentials, such as typing speed and software knowledge, or a valid driver's license and clean driving record for someone who is going to do deliveries for you. (See the sample job description on page 65.)

Next, you need to establish a pay scale. Ranges vary by parts of the country and skill level required. In Irvine, California, Cindy P. pays $11 to $14 per hour for employees whose primary responsibility is word processing. Bill P. says the highest rate he's paid in Iowa City, Iowa, is $9 per hour, and the lowest is minimum wage (to an employee who wasn't a particularly fast typist but who was accurate and reliable). You can get a good idea of the pay ranges in your area simply by checking the classified ads in your local paper.

You'll also need a job application form. You can get a basic form at most office supply stores, or you can create your own. In any case, have your attorney review the form you'll be using for compliance with the most current employment laws.

Every prospective employee should fill out an application—even if it's someone you know, and even if they have submitted a detailed resume. A resume is not a signed, sworn statement acknowledging that you can fire them if they lie; an application is. The application will also help you verify their resume; compare the two and make sure the information is consistent.

Now you're ready to start looking for candidates.

Looking in the Right Places

Picture the ideal candidate in your mind. Is this person likely to be unemployed and reading the classified ads? It is possible, but you will probably improve your chances for a successful hire if you are more creative in your search techniques than simply writing a "help wanted" ad.

Sources for prospective employees include suppliers, former co-workers, customers, and professional associations. Check with nearby colleges and perhaps even high schools for part-time help. Put the word out among your social contacts as well—you never know who might know the perfect person for your operation. "It's incredibly difficult to find good people," says Cindy P. Chicago's Joann V. agrees; she says word-of-mouth works best for her as a recruiting tool, particularly with home-based independent contractors.

Use caution if you decide to hire friends and relatives—many personal relationships are not strong enough to survive an employee-employer situation. Small-business owners in all industries tell of nightmarish experiences when a friend or relative

---

Job Description

Position: Typist/Transcriptionist

Duties: Word processing and transcription; occasionally answer telephone and greet clients; interact with clients as necessary to clarify and complete work

Required skills: Minimum typing speed of 70 words per minute; proficient in Microsoft Word; able to operate transcription machine; knowledge of punctuation and grammar; and the ability to proofread

---

refused to accept direction or in other ways abused a personal relationship in the course of business.

The key to success as an employer is making it clear from the start that you are the one in charge. You don't need to act like a dictator, of course. Be diplomatic, but set the ground rules in advance and stick to them.

Evaluating Applicants

When you actually begin the hiring process, don't be surprised if you're as nervous at the prospect of interviewing potential employees as they are about being interviewed. After all, they may need a job—but the future of your company is at stake.

It's a good idea to prepare your interview questions in advance. Develop open-ended questions that encourage the candidate to talk. In addition to knowing *what* they've done, you want to find out *how* they did it. Ask each candidate for a particular position on the same set of questions, and take notes as they respond so you can make an accurate assessment and comparison later.

You also need to evaluate their skills. Have them take a standard typing test to measure their speed. How fast you will require them to type is a judgment call you must make, and it will be based in great part on the particular work they'll be doing. For example, someone who will spend most of their time doing desktop publishing and

Smart Tip

Tip...

A great place to look for part-time employees or independent contractors is among full-time secretarial/administrative professionals who might want to do some work on the side to earn extra money. These workers are most likely to be available at night and on weekends, which lets you expand the scope and speed of your services. Find them by networking among people you know and putting the word out through local professional associations.

page layout doesn't need to be a fast typist, but speed and accuracy is critical for a transcriptionist.

Joann V. insists on a minimum typing speed of 75 words per minute for her transcriptionists even though she pays by the page. She says, "When you get paid by the page, if you're under that, you don't make enough money for yourself. If you're at 75 words per minute, you're going to make approximately $12 an hour. A lot of my transcriptionists are at 90 words per minute and above, so they make about $15 an hour."

You should also administer a test to assess candidates' grammar and punctuation skills. You can either make up your own test or purchase tests through commercial testing firms or human resources consultants.

You'll also want to confirm each candidate's familiarity with the software you use. In most cases, it won't be essential that they know your programs; if they have basic computer skills, it shouldn't take them long to learn new same-purpose software. For example, if they know Microsoft Word, they'll likely be able to pick up Corel's WordPerfect fairly quickly, and they should be able to do that using the software publisher's tutorials or other commercial training products.

You probably won't want to invest the time and money in training a new hire on more complex programs such as ones that do spreadsheets or desktop publishing. Insist that candidates who are going to be working on these types of programs demonstrate their proficiency. Get them to talk about the software, ask them to show you projects they've completed using those programs, and give them a small project they can do as a test.

Don't accept what candidates put on their resume or application at face value; interview and test to be sure they have the skill level necessary to produce the quality of work you want for your clients. "I get resumes from people who say they have all this computer experience, and they come in and can't even turn on the machine," says Cindy P.

When the interview is over, let the candidate know what to expect. Is it going to take you several weeks to interview other candidates, check references, and make a decision? Will you want the top candidates to return for a second interview? Will you call the candidate, or should they call you? This is not only a good business practice; it's also just simple common courtesy.

Always check former employers and personal references. Though many companies are very restrictive as to what information they'll verify, you may be surprised at what

> **Beware!**
> Be honest with candidates about the work they're going to be doing. Don't mislead them and insist that they'll be working on exciting, challenging projects if in reality they'll spend most of their time typing materials they find boring. Of course, if the work is truly interesting—as is much of the transcribing Joann V.'s Chicago company does—use that fact as a recruiting tool.

Who's Who?

Some of the projects you'll do will require little more than strong typing skills and an awareness of spelling and grammar; other projects will require some very specific expertise. Also, as your company grows, you'll want to consider hiring people to handle management and marketing for your firm. Here is a sample of the workers you may need:

○ *Typist/word processor.* This is the foundation of your staff, the person who does the bulk of the work by typing documents, transcribing tapes, and doing other data entry work.

○ *Secretary/administrative assistant.* For both yourself and your clients, this individual types and handles other administrative chores.

○ *Receptionist/telephone operator.* This person will greet visitors, direct calls and take messages for your business as well as for your clients if you're in an executive suite situation or if you offer telephone answering as part of your service package.

○ *Graphic designer.* This is the creative person who does page layout and design for your clients' brochures, newsletters, presentations, and other materials.

○ *Editor/proofreader.* Checking copy for accuracy and clarity is this person's critical function and special talent.

○ *Office manager.* As your business grows, you may want to turn the day-to-day running of the office over to a manager.

○ *Supervisor.* Depending on the size of your staff, you may need one or more supervisors or team leaders to adequately direct and supervise the workload.

○ *Sales/marketing rep.* As the business owner, you'll do the majority of sales and marketing, especially in the beginning. However, as your company grows, you may want to hire someone to generate new business on a part-time or full-time basis.

you can find out. Certainly you should at least confirm that the applicant told the truth about dates and positions held. Personal references are likely to give you some additional insight into the general character and personality of the candidate; this will help you decide if they'll fit into your operation.

Keep in mind that under the Immigration Reform and Control Act of 1986, you may only hire persons who may legally work in the United States, which means citizens and nationals of the United States, and aliens authorized to work in the U.S. As an employer, you must verify the identity and employment eligibility of everyone you hire. During the interviewing process, let the applicant know that you'll be doing this. Once you have made the job offer and the person is brought on board, you must complete the Employment Eligibility Verification Form (I-9) and then retain it for at least three years, or one year after employment ends, whichever period of time is longer.

Be sure to document every step of the interview and reference-checking process. Even very small companies are finding themselves targets of employment discrimination suits; if it happens to you, good records are your best defense.

Smart Tip

Training employees—even part-time, temporary help—in your way of doing things is important. They represent your company and need to know how to maintain the image and standards you've worked hard to establish.

Once They're on Board

The hiring process is only the beginning of the challenge of having employees. The next thing you need to do is train them.

Many small businesses conduct their "training" just by throwing someone into the job, but that's not fair to the employee, and it's certainly not good for your business. If you think you can't afford to spend time on training, think again—can you afford *not* to adequately train your employees? Do you want your employees working on projects or interacting with your clients when you haven't told them how you want things done?

In an ideal world, employees could be hired already knowing everything they need to know. But this isn't an ideal world, and if you want the job done right, you have to teach your people how to do it.

Whether done in a formal classroom setting or on the job, effective training begins with a clear goal and a plan for reaching it. Training falls into one of three categories: orientation, which includes explaining company policies and procedures; job skills, which focuses on how to do specific tasks; and ongoing development, which enhances basic job skills and grooms employees for future challenges and opportunities. These tips will help you maximize your training efforts:

- *Find out how people learn best.* Delivering training is not a one-size-fits-all proposition. People absorb and process information differently, and your training method needs to be compatible with their individual preferences. Some people can read a manual, others prefer a verbal explanation, and still others need to see a demonstration.

- *Be a strong role model.* Don't expect more from your employees than you are willing to do. You're a good role model when you do things the way they should be done all the time. Don't take shortcuts you don't want your employees to take or behave in any way you don't want them to behave. On the other hand, don't assume that simply doing things the right way is enough to teach others how to do things. Role-modeling is not a substitute for training; it reinforces training. If you only role-model but never train, employees aren't likely to get the message.

- *Look for training opportunities.* Once you get beyond basic orientation and job skills training, you need to constantly be on the lookout for opportunities to enhance the skill and performance levels of your people.

- *Make it real.* Whenever possible, use real-life situations to train—but avoid letting clients know they've become a training experience for employees.

- *Anticipate questions.* Don't assume that employees know what to ask. In a new situation, people often don't understand enough to formulate questions. Anticipate their questions and answer them in advance.

- *Ask for feedback.* Finally, encourage your employees to let you know how you are doing as a trainer. Just as you evaluate their performance, convince them that it's OK to tell you the truth, ask your employees what they thought of the training and your techniques, and use that information to improve your own training skills.

Employee Benefits

The actual wages you pay may be only part of your employees' total compensation. While many very small companies do not offer a formal benefits program, more and more business owners have recognized that benefits—particularly in the area of insurance—are extremely important when it comes to attracting and retaining quality employees. In most parts of the country, the employment rate is higher than it's been in decades, which means competition for good people is stiff.

Typical benefits packages include group insurance (your employees may pay all or a portion of their premiums), paid holidays, and vacations. Some services offer year-end bonuses based on the company's profitability. You can build employee loyalty by seeking additional benefits that may be somewhat unusual—and they don't have to cost much. For example, if you're in a retail location, talk to other store owners in your shopping center to see if they're interested in providing reciprocal employee discounts. You'll not only provide your own employees with a benefit, but you may get some new customers out of the arrangement.

One type of insurance may not be optional. In most states, if you have three or more employees, you are required by law to carry workers' compensation insurance.

> **Tip...**
>
> **Smart Tip**
>
> No matter how much you enjoy your work, you need an occasional break from it, whether it's to take a vacation or to deal with an illness or personal emergency. Be sure your employees and subcontractors are well-trained and committed to maintaining your service levels whether you are there or not.

This coverage pays medical expenses and replaces a portion of the employee's wages if he or she is injured on the job. Although the chances of such an injury are low in this industry, even if you have only one or two employees, you may want to consider this coverage to protect both them and you in the event of an accident, or if they develop any physical problems related to repetitive motion, such as carpal tunnel syndrome from typing.

Details and requirements vary by state; contact your state's insurance office or your own insurance agent for information so you can be sure to be in compliance.

Bright Idea

If you have employees, consider using a payroll service rather than trying to handle this task yourself. The service will calculate taxes; handle reporting and paying local, state, and federal payroll taxes; make deductions for savings, insurance premiums, loan payments, etc.; and may offer other benefits to you and your employees.

Beyond tangible benefits, look for ways to provide positive working conditions. Consider flexible working hours, establish family-friendly policies, and be sure the physical environment is comfortable and designed to enhance productivity.

Independent Contractors

The business support service industry is very conducive to working with independent contractors, either on an hourly or per-project basis. From an administrative perspective, independent contractors are much easier to deal with than employees—you simply pay them for the work they do, and they're responsible for their own taxes, benefits, etc.

It's important to build a relationship with your independent contractors, just as you would with employees. Although they will typically work from home, get to know them and make them feel like a valued member of your team.

It's also a good idea to have them sign an agreement that defines your relationship, confirms their independent contractor status, establishes work standards, and addresses confidentiality and competitive issues. For example, Joann V.'s agreement requires typists to delete any client data from their computers within 30 days of completing the project and prevents them from discussing client work with anyone outside the firm. You'll also want to prohibit independent contractors from by-passing you and going directly to your clients to get the work.

Joann has transcriptionists who have worked for her as independent contractors for as long as ten years. "They pick and choose the projects and how much they want to work," she says. "I have some who make $250 every two weeks and some who make $2,000. It's totally up to them."

It's also important to be sure your independent contractors meet the requirements set by the IRS.

Choosing the Right Equipment

Having the right equipment is a critical part of being able to provide the services your clients want and need. On the plus side, compared with many other types of businesses, your equipment needs are minimal. However, choosing the right pieces for your particular operation will take some research.

▲

Chances are, you find a trip to your local office supply superstore more exciting than a day at the mall, but resist the temptation to get carried away with exotic gadgets and "office toys." Think carefully about what you need—and don't need—do your homework, and make your buying decisions wisely.

Computers and Related Equipment

Here's a quick rundown of the basic equipment you'll most likely need.

- *Computer*. Your computer is the foundation of your business support service, and it will also help you manage bookkeeping and inventory control tasks, calculate estimates, coordinate workloads, maintain customer records, and produce marketing materials. You don't necessarily need the "latest and greatest" in computer power, but you need a system with at least Windows 98 or XP, a Pentium processor, 32 to 48MB RAM, a minimum 3GB hard drive, a CD or DVD, and a 33.6K modem. Expect to spend $1,500 to $3,500 for your computer.

- *Printer*. There was a time when your choice of printers was simple: If you wanted to provide quality, you had to have a laser printer. But as inkjet technology improves and prices drop, you may be able to meet your clients' needs with a lower-priced printer. This is a judgment call you have to make, depending on the type of work you do and the quality of output you need. Points to consider include whether your clients want color output, high-density camera-ready output (for desktop-publishing projects) or if simple, good-quality black-and-white printing will suffice. You'll likely spend $200 to $1,000 for your printer.

- *Software*. Think of software as your computer's "brains," the instructions that tell your computer how to accomplish the functions you need. You'll need a major word-processing program, such as Microsoft Word or WordPerfect, that can read and convert files created in other formats. It's important to stay reasonably current on the version of your software; most of

Got the Goods?

On the subject of equipment, there are a couple of issues you need to think about carefully before making the final decision on what to buy—and how to pay for it.

○ *Used or new.* Most of the operators we talked with preferred to buy new when it comes to computers, printers, and other equipment used in the delivery of their services. Though used equipment is usually a bargain from a price perspective, the technology is often out of date. Chicago's Joann V. says she has had a problem with used transcription units working reliably. "I'm at the point where I will buy nothing used, especially computers, because the technology changes so rapidly," she says. Janet S. in Edmond, Oklahoma, agrees, saying, "The price may be much cheaper, but the reliability of used equipment is not worth the money saved." Furnishings such as desks, chairs, filing cabinets, and various office fixtures are a different story. These items can safely be purchased used at a substantial savings through dealers, classified ads, and other sources.

○ *Service contracts.* The business support service operators we spoke with didn't feel service contracts were a worthwhile investment. In Winter Park, Florida, Charlene D. considered and rejected the idea of a service contract on her computer, which is her primary piece of equipment. "If it falls apart, I'll just buy a new one," she says. "The technology is changing so fast that most computers are out of date before they begin to have problems."

○ *Lease or buy.* With computers and peripherals becoming increasingly affordable, the leasing option is becoming decreasingly viable. Most leasing companies don't want to bother with a single computer-and-printer package, and business owners find it makes more financial management sense to buy the equipment.

the upgrades are not extremely expensive, and you don't want your clients thinking your equipment is antiquated.

The software you'll need beyond a good word-processing program will depend on the services you offer. If you're going to do page layout and graphic design, you'll need a good desktop-publishing program, such as PageMaker or QuarkXPress, along with some drawing and design programs. If you're going to maintain databases and mailing lists, you'll need a program designed to handle these functions; typically, they come under the "contact management software" category. For spreadsheet design, you'll need a program such as Microsoft Excel.

In addition to purchasing software to provide services to your clients, you'll also need programs that will handle your accounting, inventory, customer information management, and other administrative requirements. Software can be a significant investment, so do a careful analysis of your own needs and then study the market and examine a variety of products before making a final decision.

> **Beware!**
> Only work with legally purchased, properly licensed software, and be sure you read and understand the terms of your software agreement. For example, chances are your software agreement prohibits installation on multiple computers for multiple users unless you pay for that type of use. Law enforcement agencies are cracking down on software piracy; it's better to pay the price and operate legally and ethically than risk criminal charges.

- *Scanner.* If you are going to be doing word processing from existing documents, a scanner can be a tremendous productivity tool because it can save you hours of data entry. It will also be useful if you are doing desktop publishing and presentations because it allows you to include photographs and artwork in the documents. Expect to pay $150 to $1,000.

- *Data-backup systems.* To protect your own and your clients' electronic data, you need to routinely perform a backup. You can use tape, another hard drive, CDs, or floppy disks to store your backed-up data. Your computer vendor can help you choose a backup system compatible with your computer.

- *Uninterruptible power supply.* To protect your computer system as well as work in progress, all of your machines should be plugged into an uninterruptible power supply that will provide electricity in the event of a power failure. These devices also provide a degree of protection against power surges. Prices range from $90 to $200.

- *Modem.* Modems are necessary to access online services and the Internet and have become a standard component of most computers. If you are going to conduct any business online, whether it's creating your own Web site or sites for your clients, doing research, or simply communicating via e-mail, you must have a modem. The good news? Modems are usually included in the price of new computer systems.

One more thing you need to think about before making your final decision is whether to buy a Macintosh or a Windows-based PC. There was a time when Macs were used primarily for graphic design work and didn't have much in the way of other business software available, while Windows (and even the old DOS) systems had plenty of business software but could not handle the graphics side as well as Macs. But as both systems have evolved, the differences between them have become more personal preference than capability.

Businesses tend to use Windows-based PCs more than Macintoshes for their basic word-processing and administrative needs. When making your decision, keep in mind that your system needs to be compatible with the majority of your clients' equipment.

Other Office Equipment

There are a few other pieces of equipment that, depending on your situation, you may need.

- *Typewriter.* You may think that most typewriters are in museums these days, but they actually remain quite useful to businesses that deal frequently with pre-printed and multipart forms, such as order forms and shipping documents. Most business support services will need at least one typewriter. Cindy P.'s Irvine, California, service owns three; she says she uses them for forms, applications, and other documents that can't be completed on a computer. A good electric model can be purchased for $100 to $500.

- *Photocopier.* The photocopier is a fixture of the modern office and can be useful to even the smallest business support service. You can get a basic, low-end, no-frills personal copier for less than $400 in just about any office supply store. This will meet your needs if you're not doing a huge volume of photocopying for your clients. More elaborate models increase proportionately in price. If you anticipate a heavy volume, consider leasing. If you are located in a retail location, you may want to consider a coin-operated copy machine that is accessible to the public.

- *Fax machine.* Fax capability has become another essential of modern offices. You can either add a fax card to your computer or buy a stand-alone machine. If you use your computer, it must be on to send or receive faxes, and the transmission may interrupt other work. For most business support services, a stand-alone machine on a dedicated telephone line is a wise investment. Expect to pay $250 to $700 for a fax machine. Don't forget to consider the cost of toner cartridges and paper when evaluating a fax machine. These items can add up!

- *Dictation and transcription equipment.* If you are going to offer dictation or tape transcription services, you'll need the right equipment. The dictation system you buy will depend on how sophisticated you want to be and the needs of your clients. In most cases, this will not be a start-up item. Transcription machines typically handle micro, mini, and standard cassettes; which size you get will depend on the size tapes your clients use. Expect to pay from $150 to $300 for a transcription machine.

- *Postage scale.* Unless all of your mail is identical, and especially if you are going to be mailing materials for your clients, a postage scale is a valuable investment. An accurate scale takes the guesswork out of postage and will quickly pay for itself. It's a good idea to weigh every piece of mail to eliminate the risk of items being returned for insufficient postage or overpaying when you're unsure of the weight. Light mailers—one to 12 articles per day—will be adequately served by inexpensive mechanical postal scales, which typically range from $10 to $25. If you are averaging 12 to 24 items per day, consider a digital scale, which is somewhat more expensive—generally from $50 to $200—but significantly more accurate than a mechanical unit. If you send more than 24 items per day or use priority or expedited services frequently, you may want to invest in an electronic computing scale that weighs the item and then calculates the rate via the carrier of your choice, making it easy for you to make comparisons. The availability of a high-quality postage scale can be a competitive advantage if you handle mailings for your clients. Programmable electronic scales range from $80 to $250.

- *Postage meter.* Postage meters allow you to pay for postage in advance and print the exact amount on the mailing piece when it is used. Many postage meters can print in increments of one-tenth of a cent, which can add up to big savings for bulk mail users. Meters also provide a "big company" professional image, are more convenient than stamps, and can save you and your clients money in a number of ways.

  Postage meters are leased, not sold, with rates starting at about $30 per month. They require a license that is available from your local post office. Only four manufacturers are licensed by the United States Postal Service to manufacture and lease postage meters; your local post office can provide you with contact information.

- *Paper shredder.* A response to both a growing concern for privacy and the need to recycle and conserve space in landfills, shredders are becoming increasingly common in both homes and offices. They allow you to efficiently destroy incoming unsolicited direct mail, as well as sensitive internal documents and drafts of clients' work before they are discarded. Shredded paper can be compacted much more tightly than paper tossed in a wastebasket, which conserves landfill space. Light-duty shredders start at about $25, and heavier-capacity shredders run $150 to $500.

- *Credit and debit card processing equipment.* This could range from a simple imprint machine to an online terminal. Consult with several merchant status providers to determine the most appropriate and cost-effective equipment for your business.

Telecommunications

The ability to communicate quickly with your clients and suppliers is essential to any business. Also, if you have employees who telecommute or if you use homebased independent contractors, being able to reach them quickly is important. Advancing technology gives you a wide range of telecommunications options. Most telephone companies have created departments dedicated to small and homebased businesses; contact your local service provider and ask to speak with someone who can review your needs and help you put together a service and equipment package that will work for you. Specific elements to keep in mind include:

> **Your telephone can be a tremendous productivity tool.**

- *Telephone.* Whether you're homebased or in a commercial location, a single voice telephone line should be adequate during the start-up period. As you grow and your call volume increases, you'll add more lines. However, even if you're homebased, you should have a separate line for your business, and you may want to consider another separate line for your fax and data line.

  Your telephone itself can be a tremendous productivity tool, and most of the models on the market today are rich in features that you will find useful. Such features include automatic redial, which redials the last number you called at regular intervals until the call is completed; programmable memory for storing frequently called numbers; and a speakerphone for hands-free use. You may also want call forwarding, which allows you to forward calls to another phone number when you are not at your desk, and call waiting, which signals you that another call is coming in while you are on the phone. These services are typically available through your telephone company for a monthly fee.

  If you're going to be spending a great deal of time on the phone, perhaps doing marketing or handling customer service, consider a headset for comfort and efficiency. A cordless phone lets you move around freely while talking, but these units vary widely in price and quality, so research them thoroughly before making a purchase.

- *Answering machine/voice mail.* Because your business phone should never go unanswered, you need some sort of reliable answering device to take calls when

Office Supplies Checklist

Use this handy list as a shopping guide for equipping your office with supplies (you probably already have some of these). After you've done your shopping, fill in the purchase price next to each item, add up your costs, and you'll have a head start on estimating your start-up costs.

Items	Price
❑ Scratch pads	$_____
❑ Staplers, staples, and staple removers	$_____
❑ Tape and dispensers	$_____
❑ Scissors	$_____
❑ "Sticky" notes in an assortment of sizes	$_____
❑ Paper clips	$_____
❑ Plain paper for your copier and printer	$_____
❑ Paper and other supplies for your fax machine	$_____
❑ Letter openers	$_____
❑ Pens, pencils, and holders	$_____
❑ Correction fluid (to correct typewritten or handwritten documents)	$_____
❑ Trash cans	$_____
❑ Desktop document trays	$_____
❑ Labels	$_____
Total Office Supplies Expenditures:	$_____

you can't do it yourself. Whether you buy an answering machine (expect to pay $40 to $150 for one that is suitable for a business) or use the voice-mail service provided through your telephone company is a choice you must make depending on your personal preferences, work style, and needs.

- *Cellular phone.* Once considered a luxury, cellular phones have become standard equipment for most business owners. Most have features similar to your office phone—such as caller ID, call waiting, and voice mail—and equipment and services packages are reasonably priced.

- *Pager.* A pager lets you know that someone is trying to reach you and gives you the option of when to return the call. Many people use pagers in conjunction with cellular phones to conserve the cost of air time. Ask prospective pager suppliers if your system can be set up so you are paged whenever someone leaves a message in your voice mail; this service allows you to retrieve your messages immediately and eliminates having to periodically check to see if anyone has called. As with cellular phones, the pager industry is very competitive, so shop around for the best deal.

- *Toll-free number.* Most business support services are local operations, but if you are planning to build a large operation or are in a niche business and targeting a customer base outside your local calling area, consider a toll-free number so clients can reach you without having to make a long-distance call. Most long-distance service providers offer toll-free numbers, and they have a wide range of service and price packages. Shop around to find the best deal.

- *E-mail.* E-mail is rapidly becoming a standard element in a company's communication package and is essential for a business support service. It allows for fast, efficient, 24-hour communication and lets you transfer data and even deliver completed projects electronically. Be sure to check your messages regularly and reply to them promptly.

Reference Materials

Your clients will expect you to know or be able to find the answer to any grammar or formatting question, so a good set of reference materials is essential. You'll need a good dictionary, style guide, and desk reference. (See the Appendix in this book for suggested titles.) You'll also want to own additional reference sources, depending on the special needs of your clients. For example, if you prepare a lot of manuscripts, you'll want a guide for that. If you type research papers or reports, you'll want a good general reference book along with the guidelines of the institution(s) your clients are submitting papers to. If your target market is a particular industry, find a book that lists terminology along with presentation tips that are appropriate.

10

Marketing
Your Business

Marketing is an area where your creative side can shine. It is something many people don't like to do, but it's essential if you're going to build a successful, profitable business.

Don't be discouraged if your marketing efforts don't produce an immediate response. It's rare that someone will have a need for your services at precisely the moment you contact them, but if you put together a professional, attractive information package, they'll keep the information on file and call you when they need you—or they'll refer you to a colleague who may have the need. It's not unusual for a sales contact not to generate a response for months—or even a year.

There are issues and ideas specific to business support services that you need to know as you develop your marketing plan. For example, check with your local phone company to find out its advertising deadline and directory distribution date and, if possible, plan to launch your business in time to be included. Your Yellow Pages listing will be an important source of new business, especially in the early days, so don't get so distracted by other start-up tasks that you miss this opportunity.

Another important point is to be sure all your marketing materials are professional and letter-perfect. Many business support services that do a great job in this area for their clients often forget to do the same for themselves. Consider hiring a graphic designer and/or professional writer to help you with your marketing package; you may be able to negotiate a trade-out that will benefit you both.

Referrals Are Essential

Referrals will likely be a primary way you get new clients, so it's a good idea to have a systematic approach to the process. You should be able to identify who is mak-

---

Can I Quote You?

One of the first questions prospective clients ask will likely deal with fees. Avoid quoting a price too soon. This is a smart strategy for two primary reasons:

1. You really do need to be sure you understand the full scope of the work involved so you can quote an accurate and fair price, as well as be sure it's something you are qualified and willing to do.

2. By talking to the prospect about the work, you'll have the opportunity to impress them with your knowledge and professionalism—as well as get to know them so you can decide if they're someone you want to work with.

So when someone asks about price, simply say something like "I want to be sure the estimate I give you is accurate and complete, so before I calculate a fee, may I ask you some questions about the work?" If the client doesn't want to answer your questions, that's a red flag that this is someone who either isn't a serious prospect or will be difficult to work with.

ing referrals that ultimately turn into business so you can cultivate and reward those referral sources.

Complementary businesses are great sources of referrals. For example, print and copy shops often have customers who need word processing or desktop publishing but don't have the equipment, skills, or staff to handle these services. By doing the work well, you help them keep a client and make them look good in the process because they were smart enough to know about you.

Your referral arrangements can be set up to provide cash compensation for new business, or you may simply have an agreement where you and other cooperating businesses refer clients to each other as the need arises.

According to Lynette M. Smith, executive director of the Association of Business Support Services International, typical referral fees are 10 percent of the first six to 12 months of business from a new client; 15 percent of the first three months; or 25 percent of the first transaction only.

Of course, many referrals involve no compensation at all—satisfied clients will be happy to refer others to you simply because you do a good job. And you'll probably also get referrals from friends and associates. Charlene D. says a major portion of her Winter Park, Florida, company's business came through referrals from people at her church. "Most of my clients over the years have been either church members or people who heard about me from church members or through the church office," she says. "I did some advertising, but I didn't get any results from that. It's all been referrals, most of them directly or indirectly through the church."

You should also build a solid network of referral sources so that when your clients need something you don't do, you have someone you can refer them to. This makes life easier for your clients, who will appreciate you more for it. It also builds a relationship with your referral sources, who will likely return the favor when they can—and may even pay you a referral fee.

Charlene D. keeps a list of people who provide various business support services so she can give referrals if someone calls with a project she can't handle herself. "I don't expect any sort of referral fee—I'm more concerned with trying to make sure people get their work done," she says.

Advertising

Advertising is a great way to bring in new business, but choosing effective media may take some experimentation. Probably the single best place to advertise is in your local Yellow Pages, because that's where people look when they need a service and don't know who to call.

Many communities have more than one telephone directory publisher, so you may need to do some research to determine which directory (or directories) should carry

> ⚠ **Beware!**
> Not every "Yellow Pages" is a local telephone directory your prospective customers use. Industry-specific or geographic directories produced by independent publishers are rarely worth the cost of the ad. Think about where you look when you need something. Better yet, do a survey of your business associates and prospective clients asking them which telephone directory they would use when looking for a service such as the one you provide.

your listing and ad. Bill P. says his Iowa City, Iowa, community has two telephone directories, and he advertises in both.

Don't limit yourself to the telephone directory. Bill does some radio ads on a local news and talk station, and although he can't credit much specific new business to them, he says his current customers do hear and mention the spots. "It's only $100 to $150 per month, and I figure it's worth it to keep my name alive with current customers," he says. He also places ads in the university newspaper classified section and gets a good response from that.

In Chicago, Joann V. limits her advertising to the Yellow Pages, one trade journal, and a semiannual direct-mail campaign. She used to buy a mailing list for her direct-mail efforts, but she has found it more effective to build her own list using the telephone directory (using the listing categories of her target market) and trade journals (pulling prospects from ads and editorial mentions) as a resource. "We send a brochure and a Rolodex card, with an introduction, prices, and a toll-free number," she says. "The Rolodex card is really useful, because if they don't use it right away, they generally hang onto it. I've gotten calls years later." See the sample direct-mail letter on the next page.

Knocking on Doors

For many people, one of the most difficult things about being in business is getting out there and making sales calls—but it's a very effective way to bring work through the door. "The thing that grew my business the most was just cold-calling—having the guts to call attorneys and talk to whoever would talk to me," says Cindy P. in Irvine, California. Was the inevitable rejection hard to handle? Sure, she says, but "I didn't care, I just kept doing it. I needed the business."

One of the simplest ways to build business and set yourself apart from the competition is to just get out there and be visible. Knock on doors, hand out brochures, go to networking events—do whatever it takes to

> **Bright Idea**
> Want to try advertising but don't want to spend the money? Ask the print publication or radio station if you can negotiate a trade-out, where you provide services they need (such as word processing or typesetting) in return for ad space.

Direct-Mail Letter

March 18, 200x

Mr. John Doe
Fawnskin Insurance Co.
123 Deer Lane, Suite A
Bucktown, WA 45678

Dear Mr. Doe,

Do you need administrative assistance but don't have enough volume to justify a full-time employee? Do you occasionally have special projects your staffers don't have time to handle? Or do you periodically need a level of software or Internet expertise that you don't have in-house?

ABC Secretarial is the answer. We'll take the overload and special projects off your shoulders so you can concentrate on running and growing your business. Our full line of services includes:

- word processing
- spreadsheets
- mailing list management
- desktop publishing
- Internet services

Put us on your team, and together we'll both win. The enclosed brochure tells you more about the specific services we provide. I'll be delighted to meet with you at your convenience to discuss how we can help you.

Cordially,

Jane Smith

Jane Smith
President

P.S. Can't think of a need right now? Put the enclosed Rolodex card in your files and keep us in mind should something come up in the future.

make sure people know about your company and understand what you do.

You can make your calls on the telephone or in person. If you're targeting a small business, ask to speak to the owner. In a larger operation, the human resources manager may be a good place to start. Depending on your own target market, you could ask to speak to the sales manager with the goal of providing administrative support services to the sales staff.

Present your services concisely from the perspective of what they can do for the client. Hand them a brochure and business card (or mail these if you've called on the phone), and ask if you can help them in any way.

> ## Bright Idea
> Give your business card to everyone! In fact, give them two—one to keep, and one to share. It's much easier for someone to make a referral if they can just pass your card along. Wherever you are, whether it's a business or social situation, offer your card when you are introduced. This ensures people know your name, what you do, and how to reach you—and will remember it.

You must also stay visible with your existing clientele. You need to keep reminding them that you are the best game in town, so remember to thank them for their business and make sure you're doing everything they want and need.

Trade Shows and Seminars

If you're marketing to other businesses, it will be worth your while to attend trade shows. There are two types of shows—consumer (which focus on home, garden, and other consumer themes) and business-to-business (where exhibitors market their products and services to other companies). Focus on the business-to-business shows.

> ## Smart Tip
> Tip...
>
> Ask every new client how they found out about you. Make a note of where they heard about you and what kind of business they represent. This will let you know how well your various marketing efforts are working. You can then decide to increase certain programs and eliminate those that either aren't working or are attracting a type of business you don't want.

You don't need to exhibit; in fact, putting together a strong trade show exhibit is probably beyond the budget of most small business support services. But use the shows as a networking opportunity. Stop at each booth with the idea that the exhibitor is a prospective client; if the product is not something you'd ever buy, pick up the salesperson's business card and move on. Remember that exhibitors pay a substantial amount of money to set up at a show, and they're there to get business, not buy services. Don't waste their time on the exhibit floor if you're not a prospect for them; make your own sales contact later.

Many shows have refreshment areas and scheduled networking events where you can mix and mingle with exhibitors and other attendees. This is a good opportunity to acquire business cards of potential clients.

Don't just stuff the cards into your pocket; when you can, make a few notes on the card to remind yourself of who the person was and whether or not they indicated any need for your services.

After the show, use the cards you collected as sales leads. Send out a letter and/or a brochure (don't bother to take brochures to the show), and then follow up with a telephone call.

Be sure to take plenty of your own business cards. It's a good idea to wear a dress or suit with pockets, put your own business cards in your left pocket, and reserve your right pocket for the cards you collect. That way, you won't risk accidentally giving away someone else's card. And speaking of dress, wear business clothes—just because the show is held at a resort doesn't mean you should dress like you're on vacation. But remember that you'll likely be on your feet all day, so wear comfortable shoes. Don't chew gum or smoke, and avoid alcohol even at cocktail parties—you're there to make a good impression and get new business, not to play.

To find out about shows in your area, call your local chamber of commerce or convention center and ask for a calendar.

Another very effective marketing technique which can be used in conjunction with trade shows or as a separate effort is to offer free seminars and workshops to your prospective clients. Focus, of course, on some of the services you provide, such as writing a resume, putting together a newsletter, or doing effective direct-mail marketing. You can present your information through local business and civic organizations, churches or schools (adult vocational centers, community colleges, and even private institutions) at virtually no cost, and the host group handles the publicity and promotion.

Though it may sound self-defeating to teach people how to do for themselves what you'd really like to do for them for a fee, it isn't. Many people will listen to your advice, realize the work is too challenging for them, call you to do it for them, and happily pay you. Or they may refer someone else to you.

Reading the Classifieds

One of the best ways to find clients is to read the "help wanted" section of your local newspaper, says Rachelle Y. in Perrysburg, Ohio. "I had a brochure, a resume, and references," she says. She would answer ads for secretarial and administrative assistant positions. "If the ad said anything about answering phones or doing receptionist work, I didn't answer it, because that would have required someone to be on-site. But if they wanted someone to do work on a computer, I responded."

In answering the ad, she would suggest that perhaps the company would be better off outsourcing the work rather than hiring someone. She says many companies looking for full-time administrative or clerical help may be able to use you instead, either while they find and train an employee or instead of hiring an employee. Respond to the ad by sending a cover letter with your marketing materials, and then follow up with a telephone call. Point out the advantages of using your service—experience, skill, reliability, affordability (after all, they only pay you for what you do—not a salary that continues whether you're working or not)—and ask if they have a small project you could handle (for a fee, of course) as a demonstration of your services.

Financial Management

One of the primary indicators of the overall health of your business is its financial status, and it's important that you monitor your financial progress closely. The only way you can do that is to keep good records. You can handle the process manually or use any of the excellent computer accounting software programs on the market. You might want to ask your accountant for assistance getting your system of books set up. The key is to get set up and keep your records current and accurate throughout the life of your company.

Keeping good records helps generate financial statements that tell you exactly where you stand and what you need to do next. The key financial statements you need to understand and use regularly are:

- *Profit and loss statement (also called the P&L or income statement).* This illustrates how much your company is making or losing over a designated period—monthly, quarterly, or annually—by subtracting expenses from revenue to arrive at a net result, which is either a profit or a loss. For a sample P&L statement, turn to page 91.

- *Balance sheet.* A table showing your assets, liabilities, and capital at a specific point. A balance sheet is typically generated monthly, quarterly, or annually when the books are closed.

- *Cash flow statement.* Summarizes the operating, investing and financing activities of your business as they relate to the inflow and outflow of cash. As with the profit and loss statement, a cash flow statement is prepared to reflect a specific accounting period, such as monthly, quarterly, or annually.

Successful business support service owners review these reports regularly, at least monthly, so they always know where they stand and can move quickly to correct minor difficulties before they become major financial problems. If you wait until November to figure out whether or not you made a profit in February, you won't be in business for long. But monitoring your financial progress takes discipline, particularly when you're growing fast and working hard. If you don't do it, warns Irvine, California's Cindy P., you'll find yourself at the end of the year with nothing to show for your hard work not knowing how to improve your profitability the following year.

"You need to figure out what jobs make you money and what jobs don't," she says. "Profitability analysis should be an ongoing process, and you should track every job and know which ones are profitable and which ones are not, and stop doing the work you don't make money on."

Setting Credit Policies

When you extend credit to someone, you are essentially providing them with an interest-free loan. You wouldn't expect someone to lend you money without getting information from you about where you live and work, and your ability to repay. It just makes sense that you would want to get this information from someone you are lending money to.

Reputable companies will not object to providing you with credit information, or even paying a deposit on large projects. If you don't feel comfortable asking for at least part of the money upfront, just think how uncomfortable you'll feel if you do the work and deliver a major project and don't get paid at all. You might feel awkward asking

Profit and Loss Statement

ABC Secretarial Service
January 200x–December 200x

Income	
Sales	$85,950
Total Income	**$85,950**
Expenses	
Bank service charges	$300
Dues and subscriptions	450
Insurance	1,000
Licenses and permits	75
Office supplies	1,025
Payroll	58,000
Professional fees	850
Rent	6,000
Telephone	1,200
Utilities	2,200
Total Expenses	**$71,100**
Net Income (Profit)	**$14,850**

for a deposit or insisting on a complete credit application—until the first time you get burned. Then it will be easy.

Cindy P. does not extend credit to one-time clients. Companies that want to establish an ongoing relationship with her are asked to fill out a credit application. New clients or clients who don't meet her credit requirements pay by the project when they pick up the work. If that's inconvenient, they can pay in advance by posting a deposit. "They can give us a deposit and work it down," she says.

Joann V. in Chicago is far more lenient. "As long as they have a company name, address, and phone listing, I'll extend credit," she says. "If they come in off the street, I won't take a personal check; I insist on a company check."

Extending credit involves some risk, but the advantages of judiciously granted credit far outweigh the potential losses. Extending credit promotes customer loyalty. People will call you over a competitor because they already have an account set up and it's easy for them. Customers also often spend money more easily when they don't have to pay cash. Finally, if you ever decide to sell your business, it will have a greater value because you can show steady accounts.

Typically, you will only extend credit to businesses. Individuals will likely pay cash (or by check) at the time of purchase, or use a credit card. You need to decide how much risk you are willing to take by setting limits on how much credit you will allow each account. Also, it's a good idea to check the account status when accepting a project from

> **Bright Idea**
> Photocopy checks before depositing them. That way, if a collection problem occurs later, you have the client's current bank information in your files—that makes collecting on a judgment much easier.

a client on open credit. If the account is past due or the balance is unusually high, you may want to negotiate different terms before increasing the amount owed.

Your credit policy should include a clear collection strategy. Do not ignore over-due bills; the older a bill gets, the less likely it will ever be paid. Be prepared to take action on past-due accounts as soon as they become past due.

Billing

If you're extending credit to your customers—and it's likely you will if your clients are businesses rather than individuals—you need to establish and follow sound billing procedures.

Coordinate your billing system with your customers' payable procedures. Candidly ask what you can do to ensure prompt payment; that may include confirming the correct billing address and finding out what documentation is required to help the customer determine the validity of the invoice. Keep in mind that many large companies pay certain types of invoices on certain days of the month; find out if your customers do that,

Taxing Matters

Businesses are required to pay a wide range of taxes, and business support services are no exception. Keep good records so you can offset your local, state, and federal income taxes with the expenses of operating your company. If you sell supplies, even in small quantities, you'll probably be required by your state to charge and collect sales tax. If you have employees, you'll be responsible for paying payroll taxes. If you operate as a corporation, you'll have to pay payroll taxes for yourself; as a sole proprietor, you'll pay self-employment tax. Then there are property taxes, taxes on your equipment and inventory, fees and taxes to maintain your corporate status, your business license fee (which is really a tax), and other lesser-known taxes. Take the time to review all of your tax liabilities with your accountant.

Beware!
Including fliers or brochures with your invoices is a great marketing tool, but remember that adding an insert may cause the envelope to require extra postage. Getting the marketing message out is probably worth the extra few cents in mailing costs; just be sure you check the total weight before you mail so your invoices aren't returned to you for insufficient postage—or worse, delivered "postage due."

and schedule your invoices to arrive in time for the next payment cycle.

Most computer bookkeeping software programs include basic invoices. If you design your own invoices and statements, be sure they are clear and easy to understand. Detail each item, and indicate the amount due in bold with the words "Please pay" in front of the total. A confusing invoice may get set aside for clarification, and your payment will be delayed.

Most of the operators we talked with find it practical to issue an invoice as each project is completed and often include the invoice with the finished work. That's when customer appreciation is highest, and when they're thinking about you in a positive way, they're more likely to process your invoice quickly. If necessary, send out monthly statements summarizing what amounts are outstanding.

Finally, use your invoices as a marketing tool. Print notices of new services or reminders of services your clients may not be fully using on them. For example, after you list the items you are billing for, you might add a line that reads "We offer full mailing list management services; call us for details" or "Can't keep up with maintaining your Web page? Let us do it for you." You can also add a flier or brochure to the envelope—even though the invoice is going to an existing customer, you never know where your brochures will end up.

Checking It Twice

Just because a customer passed your first credit check with flying colors doesn't mean you should never re-evaluate their credit status—in fact, you should do it on a regular basis.

Tell customers when you initially grant their credit application that you have a policy of periodically reviewing accounts so that when you do it, it's not a surprise. Remember, things can change very quickly in the business world, and a company that is on sound financial footing this year may be quite wobbly next year.

An annual re-evaluation of all customers on open account is a good idea—but if you start to see trouble in the interim, don't wait to take action. Another time to re-evaluate a customer's credit is when they request an increase in their credit line.

Some key trouble signs are a slow-down in payments, unusual complaints about the quality of your work that you weren't getting before, and difficulty getting answers to your payment inquiries. Even a sharp increase in volume could signal trouble; companies concerned that they may lose their credit privileges may try to buy on credit while they can. Pay attention to what your customers are doing; a major change in their customer base or product line is something you may want to monitor.

Take the same approach to a credit review as you do to a new credit application. Most of the time, you can use what you have on file to conduct the check, but if you're

Bright Idea

Any of the popular off-the-shelf business bookkeeping and financial management software packages can help you maintain your financial records and handle billing and accounts payable.

concerned for any reason, you may want to ask the customer for updated information.

Most customers will understand routine credit reviews and accept them as a sound business practice. A customer who objects may well have something to hide—and that's something you need to know.

Accepting Credit and Debit Cards

Accepting credit cards is not as common in the business support service industry as it is in other industries, such as retail and restaurants. Joann V. used to accept credit cards, but her clients weren't using the service, so she discontinued it. However, if your market includes a substantial number of individuals (resume clients, students, etc.) and even small businesses, your clients may appreciate being able to pay by credit card. It's much easier now to get merchant status than it has been in the past; in fact, these days merchant status providers are competing aggressively for your business.

To get a credit card merchant account, start with your own bank. Also check with various professional associations that offer merchant status as a member benefit. Shop around; this is a competitive industry, and it's worth taking the time to get the best deal.

Accepting Checks

Checks will likely be your most common form of payment. When you receive a check, look for several key items. Make sure the check is drawn on a local bank. Check the date for accuracy. Do not accept a check that is undated, postdated, or more than 30 days old. Be sure the written amount and numerical amount agree.

If you accept a check from an individual, ask to see identification so you can locate the customer in case you have a problem with the check. The most valid and valuable piece of identification is a driver's license. In most states, this will include the driver's picture, signature, and address. If the signature, address, and name agree with what is printed on the check, you are probably safe. If the information does not agree, ask which is accurate and record that information on the check.

Tales from
the Trenches

By now, you should know how to get started and have a good idea of what to do—and not do—in your own business support service. But nothing teaches as well as the voice of experience. So we asked established operators to tell us what has contributed to their success; here's what they had to say.

Tell Everyone about What You Do

Never miss an opportunity to tell people about what you do for a living. You never know where you will meet that next client. In Winter Park, Florida, one of Charlene D.'s best clients came from a casual conversation, during which she mentioned that she had started a word-processing service. "That person called me a few weeks later and asked if I could do some transcribing," Charlene recalls. "Later, she told me she probably wouldn't have outsourced the work to a stranger, but since she felt like she knew me, although not very well, she felt comfortable calling me. She has become a steady client, and she regularly refers other clients to me—all from one short conversation."

Thrive under Pressure

In this business, it's just one deadline after another, operators report. When one project is done, the next one is waiting, and you don't get much of a break in between. "This is a service business that involves deadlines for almost every customer," says Bill P. in Iowa City, Iowa. "Once in a while, there is somebody who says 'Call me back in a month or two when you're done,' but usually they want it yesterday. You need to be able to work well under deadline pressure."

Keep Plenty of Supplies on Hand

Always have a good stock of supplies on hand—paper, toner, and ink cartridges, labels, etc.—so you don't run out in the middle of a project. "You will run out of toner or ink at the most unexpected and inconvenient time," says Charlene D. "I learned the hard way. Once I ran out of ink in the middle of the night. Another time, I was planning to work late in the evening preparing a mailing that needed to go to the post office first thing the next morning. I thought I had more labels on hand than I did, and I ran out in the middle of the print run. I had to wait until the office supply store opened the next morning, and then finish printing the labels and preparing the mailing. I made it to the post office by the end of the day, but it was close, and it was later than the client would have preferred."

Even if you don't routinely work at night, Charlene adds, an unscheduled run to the office supply store is a serious time-waster and can affect the quality of service you give your clients. Set up a system to make sure your supplies never drop below a specific minimum level that is appropriate for your operation.

Raise Your Rates

If you're working too much but can't afford to cut back because you need the money, raise your rates. Sure, you'll probably lose a few clients, but they are the ones for whom price is more important than quality. Reasonable clients expect periodic rate increases.

Stand Up for Yourself

Charlene D. says one of her biggest challenges has been dealing with clients who are very demanding. "One of my former clients was a nonprofit group. Their staff people were extremely demanding. When I began working for them, I explained that I was only working part time from home because I had a small baby. I told them I would do a good job at reasonable rates but that my family came first—that's what I tell all my clients, and that's how I run my business. But these people just didn't seem to grasp that. They'd call and want me to drop what I was doing, run over to their office and just do things in a rush without any regard to anything else I had to do," she says. "I talked with them about my policies over and over, and they would apologize and be thoughtful for a while; then they'd get back into these same last-minute, inconsiderate patterns. I finally told them that they needed someone who didn't mind working that way and that I couldn't work for them anymore."

Although she felt the only solution with that client was to end their relationship, she says you can stand up for your rights and still preserve the client relationship in most cases. "I set reasonable boundaries and I'm upfront and honest with my clients from the very beginning," she says. "Most of the time, they can live with that. And if they can't, I don't need their business."

Expect the Unexpected

Being in business is a lot like being married: You don't know what it's really like until you do it. Irvine, California's Cindy P. says the volume of work involved in the business surprised her. "It's so much work. I thought I could go to lunch for two hours every day and nobody would notice or complain, and that I could come in late and go home early. It's not that way." She works long days, sometimes as many as 18 hours, and most weekends.

No matter how long you're in the business or how many times you think you've seen it all, there will always be something to surprise you—an off-the-wall client, a bizarre project, an erratic employee—and you might as well get used to it.

Recognize the Value of Your Clients

Once you get a client on board, it is far more efficient and profitable to keep them than to lose them and find another one. "Make sure you treat customers right," advises Bill P. "A good customer is hard to find. I've had one or two regular customers that I screwed up and lost, and you just want to kick yourself in the teeth when that happens."

Keep Your Employees
and Independent Contractors Happy

Good workers are valuable, and trend-watchers say the employment situation isn't going to change any time soon. If you find someone who produces fast, accurate work, look for ways to build loyalty so you'll retain them. Treat workers fairly and with respect, don't allow clients to abuse them, and pay them as well as you can.

Chicago's Joann V. says providing variety in their work also helps. "If they feel like they're in a rut and I can't offer them something else to work on, they'll leave. If I get someone working strictly on one contract, they're good for about six months, and then they're gone."

Get the Contract Signed
Before You Spend Any Money

Though it may not happen often, there may be times when you'll need to make special purchases (such as equipment, software, or supplies) to handle a particular project for a client. Before you invest in a project, be sure you will get the work.

"One of the greatest mistakes I've made so far is purchasing a software package to do a job for a new client," says Janet S. in Edmond, Oklahoma. "By the time I bought and installed the software, they informed me they weren't going to use my services." Though she was able to use the software for her own operation, it was still an expense she wouldn't have incurred if the client hadn't requested it.

If a project requires an investment in training, staffing, or equipment, it's not unreasonable to insist on a contract and even an advance payment before you begin the work.

It Takes Common Sense,
Steadiness, and Hard Work

Joann V. says you need to be prepared for and able to deal with a variety of personalities. "Don't get excited, don't get too angry, and stay on an even keel," she says. "Things have a tendency to work themselves out." She attributes her growth primarily to common sense. "It wasn't a lot of research or a lot of anything except hard work and common sense," she says. "I believe that if you work hard at anything and hang in there, your time will come. Be diligent and stick with it."

Appendix
Business Support Resources

They say you can never be rich enough or young enough. While these could be argued, we believe you can never have enough resources. Therefore, we present for your consideration a wealth of sources for you to check into, check out, and harness for your own personal information blitz.

These sources are tidbits, ideas to get you started on your research. They are by no means the only sources out there and they should not be taken as the ultimate answer. We have done our research, but businesses do tend to move, change, fold, and expand. As we have repeatedly stressed, do your homework. Get out and start investigating.

Associations

Association of Business Support Services International Inc. (formerly National Association of Secretarial Services Inc.), 22875 Savi Ranch Pkwy., Ste. H, Yorba Linda, CA 92887-4619, (800) 237-1462, (714) 282-9398, fax: (714) 282-8630, www.abssi.org, e-mail: abssi4you@ aol.com

Executive Suite Association, 438 E. Wilson Bridge Rd., #200, Columbus, OH 43085, (614) 431-8295, fax: (614) 431-8258, www.execsuites.org, e-mail: ESAcentral@ aol.com

International Association of Administrative Professionals (IAAP), 10502 NW Ambassador Dr., P.O. Box 20404, Kansas City, MO 64195-0404, (816) 891-6600, fax: (816) 891-9118, www.iaap-hq.org

National Notary Association, 9350 De Soto Ave., Chatsworth, CA 91311, (800) 876-6827, fax: (800) 833-1211, www.nationalnotary.org, e-mail: services@nationalnotary.org

National Resume Writers Association, www.nrwa.com, e-mail: resumepro1@aol. com

Professional Association of Resume Writers, 3637 4th St., #330, St. Petersburg, FL 33704, (800) 822-7279, (727) 821-2274, fax: (727) 894-1277, www.parw.com, e-mail: par whq@aol.com

Books

The Chicago Manual of Style: The Essential Guide for Writers, Editors, and Publishers, University of Chicago Press

Editorial Freelancing: A Practical Guide, Trumbull Rogers, Aletheia Publications, (914) 526-2873

Start Your Own Consulting Service, John Riddle, Entrepreneur Press

Entrepreneur's business start-up guide No. 1288, *Desktop Publishing Business*

Entrepreneur's business start-up guide No. 1313, *Event Planning Service*

Entrepreneur's business start-up guide No. 1237, *Information Broker*

Entrepreneur's business start-up guide No. 1392, *Medical Transcription Service*

Gregg Reference Manual, William A. Sabin, Glencoe McGraw Hill

How to Start a Home-Based Resume Business, Second Edition, Jan Melnik, CPRW, The Globe Pequot Press, (800) 962-0973, www.globe-pequot.com

How to Start a Home-Based Desktop Publishing Business, Second Edition, Louise Kursmark, The Globe Pequot Press, (800) 962-0973, www.globe-pequot.com

Industry Production Standards Guide, Fourth Edition, Association of Business Support Services International Inc.

Pricing Manual for Business Support Services, Second Edition, Association of Business Support Services International Inc.

Pricing Guide for Desktop Services, Fourth Edition, Robert Brenner, Brenner Information Group, (619) 538-0093

Pricing Guide for Web Services, Robert Brenner, Brenner Information Group, (619) 538-0093

Starting a Successful Business Support Service, Second Edition, Lynette M. Smith, Association of Business Support Services International Inc.

Straight Talk About Promoting Your Service, Association of Business Support Services International Inc.

Successful Sales Letters, Proposals, and Literature, Second Edition, Association of Business Support Services International Inc.

The World's Easiest Guide to Using the MLA: A User-Friendly Manual for Formatting Research Papers According to the Modern Language Association Style, Carol J. Amato, Stargazer Publishing Co., (714) 531-6342

Writer's Digest Guide to Manuscript Formats, Dian Dincin Buchman, Writer's Digest Books

Consultants and Other Experts

Robert S. Bernstein, Esq., Bernstein Bernstein Krawec & Wymard, P.C., 1133 Penn Ave., Pittsburgh, PA 15222, (412) 456-8100, fax: (412) 456-8135, e-mail: bob@bern steinlaw.com

Biddle & Associates Inc., OPAC testing software (software to test typing speed/ accuracy, word-processing skills, language arts, math, financial skills, spreadsheets, databases and more), 2100 Northrop Ave., #200, Sacramento, CA 95825-3937, (800) 999-0438, fax: (916) 929-3307, www.opac. com, e-mail: staff@opac.com

Credit Card Services

American Express Merchant Services, (888) 829-7302, www.americanexpress. com

Discover Card Merchant Services, (800) 347-6673

MasterCard, (914) 249-4843, www. mastercard.com

Visa, (800) VISA-311, ext. 96, www. visa.com

Publications

Fine Forms Collection (a collection of 20 award-winning forms used by ABSSI members in a wide variety of applications in the operation of their businesses), Association of Business Support Services International Inc.

OfficePro magazine, International Association of Administrative Professionals, 5501 Backlick Rd., #240, Springfield, VA 22151-3940, (703) 914-9200, fax: (703) 914-6777, e-mail: officepromag@strattonpub.com

Successful Business Support Service Owners

Charlene Davis, 4008 Waterview Loop, Winter Park, FL 32792, (407) 679-8119, e-mail: JCD4008@aol.com

Office Assistant Secretarial Service, Janet S. Helton, 452 Dauphin Ave., Edmond, OK 73034, (405) 359-0168, e-mail: jdhelton@att.net

Orange Coast Secretarial Service, Cindy Parks, 2102 Business Center Dr., #130, Irvine, CA 92612-1001, (949) 253-4625, e-mail: OCSSCindy@aol.com

Voss Transcriptions Inc., Joann Voss, 166 W. Washington St., #200, Chicago, IL 60602, (312) 346-3227, fax: (312) 346-1199, e-mail: vosstrans@aol.com

WordCare, Bill Pypes, 31½ E. Burlington St., Iowa City, IA 52240, (319) 338-3888, fax: (319) 338-8451, e-mail: WordCare@aol.com

Young's Secretarial, Rachelle Young, 1889 Lexington Dr., Perrysburg, OH 43551, (419) 874-3404

Glossary

Desktop publishing: a method used to design and produce camera-ready, typeset documents.

Electronic file: a document prepared and stored in an electronic (as opposed to paper) format.

Independent contractor: an individual who performs work on a contract basis and who is not an employee of the company for which he/she is doing the work.

Industry Production Standards (IPS): a method of measuring production output based on a "model operator" standard and used to calculate fees.

Minimum charges: the least amount you will charge, regardless of the amount of work actually done.

Notarize: to acknowledge or attest as a notary public.

Notary public: a public officer authorized to administer oaths, to attest to and certify certain types of documents, to take depositions, and to perform certain acts in commercial matters; also referred to as a notary.

Outsourcing: the business trend of contracting with outside suppliers to provide goods and services formerly produced in-house.

Resume: a summary of an individual's professional accomplishments, typically used in the job search process, which may also include personal information, community involvement, awards and recognition, and other data.

Rush rates: extra charges applied to work done in less time than your standard production period at the client's request.

Scanner: a piece of equipment that converts paper documents and images to electronic files.

Speech recognition technology: technology that allows a user to interface with a computer by speaking rather than by typing; also known as "voice recognition technology."

Spreadsheet: an accounting program for a computer; also the ledger layout modeled by such a program.

Word processing: the production of typewritten documents with automated and usually computerized typing and text-editing equipment.

Index

▲

Start-Up Guides
Books
Software

To order our catalog call 800-421-2300.
Or visit us online at smallbizbooks.com

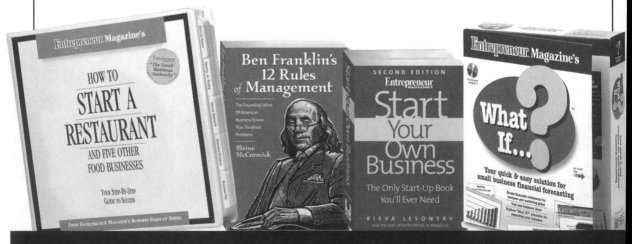